Should the United States Privatize Social Security?

Should the United States Privatize Social Security?

Henry J. Aaron and
John B. Shoven

The Alvin Hansen
Symposium
on Public Policy
Harvard University

edited and with an
introduction by
Benjamin M. Friedman

The MIT Press
Cambridge, Massachusetts
London, England

This book was set in Palatino by Achorn Graphic Services, Inc.

Printed and bound in the United States of America.

Library of Congress Cataloging-in-Publication Data

Aaron, Henry J.
    Should the United States privatize Social Security? / Henry J. Aaron and John B. Shoven : edited and with an introduction by Benjamin M. Friedman.
        p. cm.
        "The Alvin Hansen Symposium on Public Policy, Harvard University."
        Papers and discussion from the Second Alvin Hansen Symposium held on April 27, 1998.
        Includes bibliographical references and index.
        ISBN 0-262-01174-3 (alk. paper)
        1. Social security—United States—Congresses. 2. Privatization—United States—Congresses. I. Shoven, John B. II. Friedman, Benjamin M. III. Alvin Hansen Symposium on Public Policy (2nd : 1998 : Harvard University) IV. Title.
    HD7125.S535   1999
    368.4'3'00973—dc21   99-12010
                                                                CIP

Contents

5 Rejoinder   169

John B. Shoven

Introduction

Benjamin M. Friedman

Social Security is probably the most successful government program in the United States, and certainly the one most highly valued by the American public. It is also among the most threatened. Today most Americans understand that Social Security cannot continue indefinitely to pay benefits at current levels and according to current rules unless payroll taxes rise sharply. And most Americans strongly oppose significant increases in payroll taxes.

There is no secret about what has brought Social Security to this impasse. The combination of a "baby boom" following World War II and a "baby bust" a generation later created an imbalance in the American population's age structure that is now steadily reducing the number of active workers contributing to Social Security compared to the number of retirees drawing benefits. This effect is temporary, but even so it will last for decades and the problem it creates is now only beginning. At the same time, pervasive changes in medical science, in health care, and in personal health habits have significantly raised life expectancies, and therefore the number of years over which the average

American retiree will draw benefits. Unlike the effect created by the boom-then-bust in birth rates, this effect is presumably permanent. By the very nature of demographic changes, the combined implications for Social Security of these two forces have been long foreseen. Only recently, however—as the first eligibility of the oldest baby boomers for Social Security benefits (in 2007) has become close enough to appear tangible—has this much anticipated situation risen to the top of the nation's public policy agenda.

Two more recent and less anticipated developments have importantly shaped the resulting policy debate. First, the U.S. government has eliminated its budget deficit and, in the absence of new major changes in tax and spending policies, now entertains the prospect—an honest prospect—of sizeable surpluses over the next decade and beyond. And second, powerful investor confidence and strong growth in American corporations' profits over an economic expansion that has now lasted more than seven years have propelled the U.S. stock market to record highs.

The prospect of federal budget surpluses matters to the debate over Social Security in the first instance simply because it provides one possible answer to the hard question of how to "plug" the shortfall between what the system takes in from payroll taxes and what it distributes in benefit payments. But the potential availability of monies from sources other than the payroll tax also affects the Social Security debate in more far-reaching ways. In particular, this additional funding potentially makes it possible to shift Social Security from its traditional pay-as-you-go structure to a partially or even fully funded basis without otherwise requiring one age group to "pay double" to finance the transition. Whether a partially or fully funded system would be preferable to the current pay-as-you-go system has long been a matter of debate. Only now that a way to avoid the "double payment" burden is visible, however, has that debate moved from the realm of economic theory to the practical policymaking arena.

The strong performance of the U.S. stock market in recent years has affected the Social Security debate in several ways. Most obviously, it has made many Americans who have yet to retire acutely aware of how low an implicit rate of return they stand to receive from the Social Security benefits they will receive compared to the payroll taxes that they and their employers will pay. Dramatically large returns on any easily available asset (in this case equities, or equity mutual funds) highlight the appeal of potential alternative ways to finance retirement. At the same time, to the extent that Social Security itself has assets that it invests—$700 billion today, growing to $1.5 trillion (in today's dollars) by 2015—the prospect of earning a greater return than on the current portfolio, which is restricted to U.S. Treasury securities, offers a way of meeting some part of the system's demographically induced imbalance without requiring any more fundamental structural changes.

The papers offered here by Henry Aaron and John Shoven address what is perhaps the most fundamental question at issue in the current debate over what to do about Social Security: Whether to shift from the current pay-as-you-go system to one that is not just funded but, indeed, privatized in the sense that each individual participant would retain control over the investment of his or her own funded assets. The theoretical questions that have long dominated the debate over pay-as-you-go versus funding, including the likely effects on saving behavior and capital formation, figure prominently in their analyses. But so too does a broad array of important practical considerations, including those that are different today because of very recent developments in the federal budget and in the stock market.

The papers and discussion published here were presented at the second Alvin Hansen Symposium on Public Policy, held at Harvard University on April 27, 1998.[1] Questions about the structure of the U.S. Social Security System are an especially appropriate subject for a public policy symposium created in memory of Alvin Hansen. In the early 1930s, while still teaching at the University of Minnesota, Professor Hansen worked on a plan for unemployment insurance at the state level. He went on to chair a committee of technical advisors that helped structure the U.S. Social Security program, established in 1935. His central role in the hearings of the Temporary National Economic Committee in 1939, after his arrival at Harvard, gave him an opportunity to rethink several key aspects of the program's structure, and questions relating to social insurance remained in his sphere of interest in later years as well.

In introducing these proceedings, I want to express my very sincere personal thanks, as well as the gratitude of the Harvard Economics Department, to Marian Hansen Merrifield and Leroy Sorenson Merrifield, together with numerous former students of Alvin Hansen, whose generosity has made possible this series of public policy symposia that the Economics Department now sponsors at Harvard in Alvin Hansen's name. Their eager participation in this effort stands as testimony to the profound and positive effect that Professor Hansen had on so many younger economists.

I am also grateful to James Duesenberry and Richard Musgrave, who served with me on the organizing committee that established the Alvin Hansen Symposium series and then arranged the content of both of the first two symposia; to Helen Deas, who once again did a prodigious amount of work in arranging the symposium's logistics; to Terry Vaughn, for his support in bringing these proceedings to publication; and especially to Henry Aaron and John Shoven as well as our four discussants for contributing their papers and comments.

In 1967, in his eightieth year, Alvin Hansen received the American Economic Association's Francis E. Walker medal. James Tobin, in presenting this award, described him as follows:

Alvin H. Hansen, a gentle revolutionary who has lived to see his cause triumphant and his heresies orthodox, an untiring scholar whose example and influence have fruitfully changed the directions of his science, a political economist who has reformed policies and institutions in his own country and elsewhere without any power save the force of his ideas. From his boyhood on the South Dakota prairie, Alvin Hansen has believed that knowledge can improve the condition of man. In the integrity of that faith he has had the courage never to close his mind and to seek and speak the truth wherever it might lead. But Professor Hansen is to be honored with as much affection as respect. Generation after generation, students have left his seminar and his study not only enlightened but also inspired—inspired with some of his enthusiastic conviction that economics is a science for the service of mankind.

Note

1. The first Alvin Hansen Symposium, in 1995, was on "Inflation, Unemployment, and Monetary Policy," with principal papers by Robert Solow and John Taylor. The papers and discussion from that symposium have also been published by MIT Press.

1 Social Security Reform: Two Tiers Are Better Than One

John B. Shoven

Social Security is the largest federal government spending program in the United States. Most elderly depend on the program for more than half of their income and most workers pay more in Social Security payroll taxes than in personal income taxes. The program has a record of sixty years of accomplishments; perhaps, most importantly, reducing the poverty rate among the elderly to where it is today—lower than for the population as a whole. Still, Social Security faces a very uncertain economic and political future. Its Trust Fund nearly ran out of money in 1977 and then again in the early 1980s, requiring extensive changes to restore the financial soundness of the system. The last round of fixes were designed by the 1983 Greenspan Commission and included raising the payroll tax rate, advancing the normal retirement age, and partially taxing the receipt of Social Security benefits. The claim was that with the 1983 package of changes the Social Security Trust Fund would remain solvent until 2063 when the youngest baby boomer would be 100 years old. With that forecast, the Greenspan Commission could brag that it had fixed Social Security for the

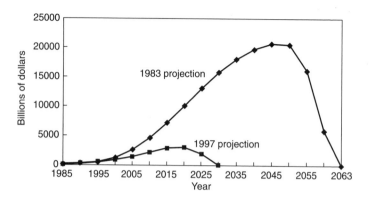

Figure 1.1
Projected OASDI trust fund accumulations in current dollars by year of estimate

baby-boom generation. Now, fifteen years later we once again hear that Social Security faces a crisis. The Greenspan Commission fix did not stick as figure 1.1, which plots the evolution of the Social Security Old Age, Survivors, and Disability Insurance (OASDI) Trust Fund as forecast in 1983 and 1997, shows graphically. The Trust Fund is now projected to run out of money in 2029 rather than 2063. For the youngest baby boomers the difference between a system with a Trust Fund that goes bankrupt when they are 100 and one that runs dry when they are 66 and just one year short of their normal retirement age (which the Commission increased to 67) makes all the difference in the world. The system needs to be redesigned once again and the question is how to do it.

This chapter tries to accomplish several things. First, I describe how Social Security works and how its structure is particularly vulnerable to financial imbalances. Second, I show that the dramatic changes in the demographic structure of the population are the reason that we have a system that is simultaneously running an annual cash-flow surplus in excess of $60 billion and yet one which is projected to fail (if not modified) in the third decade of the next century. Third, I examine the choices we face to assure Americans of their retirement security—should we engage in yet another major tuneup of the existing system, scrap it, and adopt a system of mandatory private savings accounts, or introduce a hybrid program with both government-funded benefits and supplementary individual accounts. In the end, I argue that the best policy is some kind of two-tier system. I also note that the majority of the members of the 1994–96 Advisory Council on Social Security also reached this conclusion (although they split on the specifics of which type of two-tier system) as did the Committee for Economic Development (CED). I describe the two partial privatization plans developed by the Advisory Council, the CED plan, the Moynihan-Kerry plan, the new second-generation Feldstein-Samwick plan, and one of my own that holds out the promise of financial solvency, increased benefits, and lower payroll taxes. My belief is that all of these proposals are superior to any single-tier system, be it a repaired unfunded defined benefit plan similar to the current system or a completely privatized system such as described by Feldstein and Samwick (1997) and advocated by Kotlikoff and Sachs (1997). One of the advantages of a two-tier system is simply that it doesn't put all of the retirement nest eggs in one basket. Further, hybrid systems can be designed to increase national saving, improve the financial security of workers and retirees, and provide participants with far better service, information, and rates of return than the existing Social Security program.

How Social Security Works

The existing Social Security program is basically a pay-as-you-go (PAYGO) intergenerational transfer system where each generation of workers pays a fraction of their covered earnings to Social Security, which turns around and immediately transfers most of the money to the system's beneficiaries. In return for making contributions, each worker earns the right to receive transfers from the next generation of workers when they themselves retire. If the system were a pure PAYGO plan (such as described in Samuelson [1958]) and if the contribution rate remained fixed and the population grew smoothly, then the rate of return that each generation would realize would be the sum of the population growth rate and the rate of growth of labor productivity. In that case, each generation of workers would give up a fraction of their labor earnings in return for the same fraction of the next generation's earnings. Aggregate benefits would increase in line with aggregate earnings which grow due to both an increase in the number of workers and increases in output per person.

This type of consumption-loan model hints at some of the reasons why participants in the existing U.S. Social Security system are experiencing low and decreasing rates of return on their contributions (namely the slowing rate of growth in the number of workers and the frustratingly slow rate of growth of labor productivity), but it doesn't explain the whole story. The U.S. Social Security program is not a pure

Samuelsonian intergenerational consumption loan system. Instead it is an unfunded defined benefit system and, as such, it is inherently financially unstable. Workers do not earn the right to a fraction of the next generation's earnings, rather they earn a specified retirement (inflation-indexed) life annuity. The monthly benefit that a retiree receives depends on the age of retirement (62 or later) and on the covered earnings history of the participant. The government will be able to pay the aggregate promised (i.e., defined) benefits with the legislated payroll tax rates only if the economic and demographic assumptions work out at least as favorably as forecast. A system that specifies both the precise benefits workers will receive and the future taxes workers will be asked to pay is overspecified in one dimension or the other. The system appears to be risk free (both the benefits and the taxes are legislated seventy-five years into the future), but of course participants and taxpayers bear the risks that the legislated taxes will not be sufficient to cover the promised benefits.[1] This is exactly the situation we are in now. The trustees of the Social Security System now predict that once the Trust Fund is exhausted in 2029 the system's revenues will be between two-thirds and three-fourths as much as the cost of the legislated benefits. According to today's forecast, clearly something has to give. If we wait to fix the system until the Trust Fund bankruptcy is upon us, then benefits will have to be cut or revenues increased by a total of at least one-third. "Defining" future benefits doesn't make them certain; in fact, the future benefits and payroll tax rates are uncertain—even the best actuaries cannot predict them precisely.

The Dramatically Changing Demographic Structure of the U.S. Population

The finances of an unfunded defined benefit Social Security program depend crucially on the size of aggregate labor earnings and the number of retired beneficiaries of the system. Since the program was begun in the 1930s, the normal retirement age (the age at which one can collect so-called full benefits) has been set at 65. The good news is that people who reach age 65 are living a lot longer today than they did when Social Security was originally designed. Figure 1.2 plots the remaining life expectancies for 65-year-old men and women. The parts of the graphs referring to 1940 to 1995 are based on actual data whereas the parts from 1995

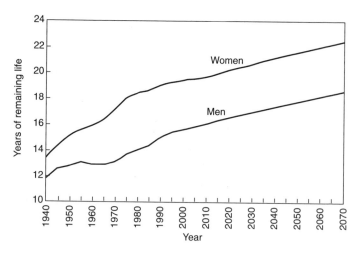

Figure 1.2
Life expectancy at age 65

to 2070 illustrate the intermediate forecast of the Census Bureau and the Social Security Administration. The life expectancies of 65-year-old men and women have improved by 3.7 and 6.1 years, respectively, since 1940 with the recent rate of improvement being a little better than one month per year for both sexes.[2] The Social Security intermediate assumption is that this rate of improvement will slow to roughly one-half month per year, although there is doubt among demographers about the likelihood of this predicted slowdown in the rate of improvement. The intermediate (or "best guess") forecast of Social Security is that the life expectancy of Americans at birth will not reach age 79 (the current life expectancy at birth in Japan) for another forty-five years (Caldwell et al. (1998)). If the recent pace of improvement were to continue, however, the mortality of Americans would equal the present mortality of Japanese in twenty years, resulting in even more severe financial pressure on the Social Security system than reflected in the intermediate forecasts. At least on the demographic variables, Social Security's high-cost assumptions may be more realistic than their intermediate ones.

The dramatic change in the ratio of the number of people of working age to the number of elderly that has occurred and is projected to occur under intermediate assumptions is shown in figure 1.3. This differs from the usual chart of workers per retiree because the decision to work is endogenous whereas one's age is fairly immutable. This chart is pure demographics. The upper line shows the number of people of working age relative to the number of elderly people if the dividing age is chosen as 70 whereas the lower line defines elderly people as those over age 65. In either

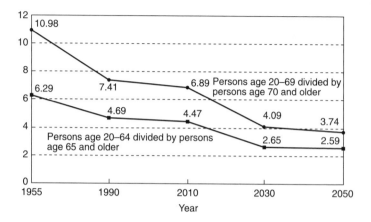

Figure 1.3
Working-age population divided by elderly population

case there is a dramatic shift in this important demographic ratio between 1990 and 2030. The number of working-age adults per elderly person declines by 47 percent between 1990 and 2030 if elderly is taken as age 70 or older (from 7.41 working-age adults per elderly person to 4.09) and by 43.5 percent if elderly is defined as being over 65 (from 4.47 to 2.65). In either case, this is a huge change in the relative size of the working age and elderly populations.

A more detailed picture of the changing demographics of the country can be seen by comparing figures 1.4 through 1.7, which show the age structure of the U.S. population in 1955, 1990, and the projected population in 2030 and 2050. These charts show the number of people alive (in millions) in different five-year-age intervals. Notice that in 1955 the country had a classic demographic pyramid with fewer and fewer people alive at the older age levels with a couple of

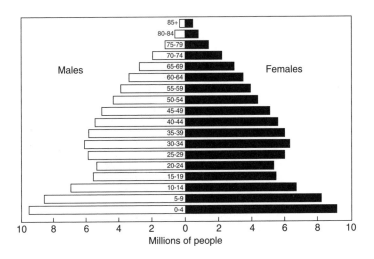

Figure 1.4
Population age structure in 1955 (in millions)

exceptions. There were relatively few people in the 15–19 and 20–24 age categories (those born in the Great Depression) and there were very large numbers of people in the 0–4 and 5–9 categories (the first of the baby boomers). Notice that those turning 65 today are among the relatively few people born in 1933. The retiring cohorts will remain relatively small for the next dozen years or so as those born in the Depression and during World War II reach age 65. This explains why Social Security is running a cash-flow surplus today even though it is insolvent in the long run. Figure 1.4 also illustrates how few people were over the age of 85 in 1955. The subsequent figures will show tremendous growth in the population of the very elderly.

Figure 1.5 shows a more recent age structure for the country, namely for 1990. The demographic bulge called the baby

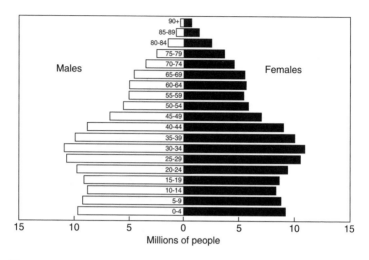

Figure 1.5
Population age structure in 1990 (in millions)

boom is very apparent. Notice also that the 85 and over category has been divided into 85–89 and 90+ categories and that there were more people over 90 in 1990 than there were over 85 in 1955. Figure 1.6 shows the projected (intermediate forecast) demographic structure for 2030, one year after the projected exhaustion of the Social Security Trust Fund and the year in which the youngest baby boomer turns 67 and becomes eligible for full benefits. There will be approximately 61.5 million people between the ages of 65 and 84 in 2030 (roughly corresponding to baby boomers). The growth in the elderly populations between 1990 and 2030 is quite dramatic. For instance, the number of men between 75 and 79 almost triples from 2.4 million to 6.7 million. The number of women over the age of 85 in 2030 exceeds the number of

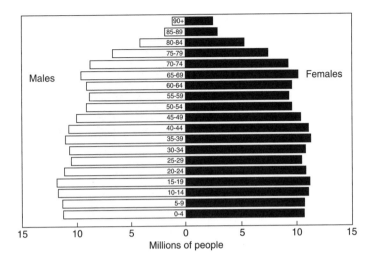

Figure 1.6
Population age structure in 2030 (in millions)

women between 55 and 59 in 1990. The demographic pyramid, so evident in 1955, is not apparent at all until after 75 years of age. Very roughly speaking, in 2030 there will be as many people between ages 65 and 74 as in any of the younger ten-year age intervals. Figure 1.7 contains the intermediate Social Security forecast for the age structure of the United States in 2050. While this may appear far into the future, the forecast is that there will still be some 17.7 million baby boomers alive in the 85 and over category.

The Greenspan Commission was right about one thing— the boomers will be around in nontrivial numbers until roughly 2063. It is also predicted that there will be more than 6 million women over the age of 90 in 2050. This compares to roughly 800,000 women in this age category today.

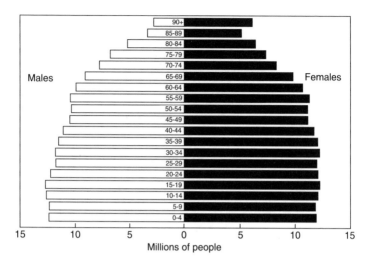

Figure 1.7
Population age structure in 2050 (in millions)

It is not at all surprising that Social Security will have to be significantly redesigned to deal with the demographic future. In considering the alternatives for repairing the finances of OASDI, it is important to keep in mind that the same demographic trends that destabilize the OASDI system contribute enormously to the growth in long-run health care costs in the United States and to Medicare's financial problems in particular. While Social Security's seventy-five year financial balance could be restored by simply raising the payroll tax rate today by approximately 2.25 percentage points, solving the long-run Medicare financial situation would require much larger payroll tax hikes if we try to fix things by simply enhancing revenues. If we wanted to address the OASDI problem through tax increases, but

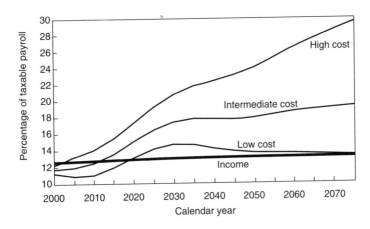

Figure 1.8
Estimated OASDI income rates and cost rates by assumption alternatives,
2000–2075

somehow do not get around to doing so for awhile, the required increase gets much more painful. Waiting for another twenty years would mean that the required increase jumps to between four and five percentage points. Finally, if we only fix it for seventy-five years, the new "fix" will immediately begin to unravel, just like the 1983 one did.

The magnitude of the emerging financial crisis for the OASDI part of Social Security is easily comprehended by examining figure 1.8. The three cost curves show the projected expenses of OASDI as a percentage of covered payroll under the three sets of economic and demographic projections examined by the trustees of the system. Usually people focus on the intermediate cost assumptions. The cost curves show how the payroll tax rate would have to evolve if the benefits of the system were to be maintained and if we adopted a strictly pay-as-you-go policy. The gap between the cost curves and the income line (it's actually a curve, but a remarkably straight one) would be the required payroll tax hikes to equate costs and revenues. As can be seen, the gap between costs and income grows rapidly after 2010 reaching 4.4 percentage points by 2030 with the intermediate set of assumptions and 7.7 percentage points under the high-cost assumption set. By 2075 the gaps are 6.1 and 16.3 percentage points, respectively. My conclusion is that there is a strong likelihood that the finances of the system will evolve somewhere between the intermediate and high-cost paths shown in figure 1.8; this means that serious steps need to be taken to close the cost and income gaps and restore Social Security to financial equilibrium. The fact that Medicare faces an even larger divergence between costs and income in the future makes it more imperative that we seriously address the OASDI problems.

Principles of Social Security Reform and Some Observations

This section lists some principles of Social Security reform that reflect what I perceive to be consensus values in the country. If accepted, they can eliminate some of the extreme proposals from serious consideration. First, let me list the principles and then elaborate on some of them.

1. The important "safety net" or redistributive features of the existing Social Security system should be preserved.
2. Any redesign of Social Security should enhance the low rate of national saving.

3. Any reform should offer long-run solvency for the system, not simply postpone insolvency.

4. Any reform should improve equity between participants (particularly between one and two earner couples).

5. Economic efficiency should be increased by increasing the link between contributions and benefits.

6. The risks borne by individual participants should be kept at tolerable levels.

7. Administrative costs should be minimized.

8. The reforms should be determined and announced as soon as possible.

I contend that we can do better in meeting all of these goals or principles if we adopt a two-part or hybrid-defined benefit and defined contribution plan than if we choose to rely exclusively on one or the other.

As noted earlier, probably the greatest accomplishment of Social Security is the reduction of incidence of poverty among the elderly. The program has a sharply progressive benefit formula (which more than offsets the regressive tax structure) with the result that low-income participants receive a higher rate of return than middle- and high-income participants. This redistribution was most recently documented in Caldwell et al. (1998). I believe that such redistribution from those with higher lifetime earnings to those with lower earnings is entirely appropriate and worth preserving.

The second principle listed above, that we should take the opportunity of Social Security reform to increase the saving rate in the country, recognizes that there is a remarkable level of agreement among economists that the U.S. saving rate is suboptimal.[3] For the last decade or more, the net U.S. national saving rate has been roughly 3 percent of gross domestic product, less than half of what the rate was in the 1950s, 1960s, and 1970s. A sustained higher national saving rate would increase the domestically owned capital stock and significantly increase real wages within the next twenty years as shown in Aaron, Bosworth, and Burtless (1989). Although there is no agreement as to the exact magnitudes, there is widespread acceptance of the fact that the PAYGO Social Security system has depressed personal and national savings. Further, providing for retirement is the most important motive for saving. Thus, we should try to increase saving while restoring the long-run solvency of Social Security.

The third principle is prompted by the 1983 reforms. Even when Congress adopted the Greenspan plan to achieve a seventy-five-year financial balance for the system, it was recognized that the mere passage of time would lead to the recurrence of a seventy-five-year shortfall. As each year passed there was one fewer surplus year at the beginning of the rolling seventy-five-year horizon and one more deficit year at the end. About one-third of today's imbalance in the seventy-five-year outlook is due to this "passage of time effect." What we should aspire to now is a system that not only is balanced over the next seventy-five years but one that appears to be workable thereafter.

Some of the transfers within the existing system are not only defensible, they are worth preserving. There are also large inequities, however, among two-earner couples, one-earner couples, and single individuals which should be rethought. There are other specific aspects of Social Security rules that appear to be convoluted and inappropriate. For instance, the cliff vesting of marriages at ten years (divorced individuals can claim benefits based on the earnings of their ex-spouse only if they were married for ten years or more) seems arbitrary. Finally, since poverty is greatest among widows, widow benefits should be increased relative to those for married couples.

The fifth principle is a very important one. There always has been a debate about whether Social Security contributions should be thought of as taxes or deferred compensation (i.e., pension contributions). The current system has a relatively weak link between marginal contributions and marginal benefits and therefore may be viewed by most people as a tax / transfer system rather than a deferred compensation pension system. For people with covered work histories shorter than ten years and for many whose careers are longer than thirty-five years, there is zero marginal benefit to additional marginal contributions. For secondary earners in two-earner households, the marginal connection between contributions and benefits is small or nil. If the full 15.3 percent payroll tax is viewed as a marginal tax with little or no offsetting marginal benefits,[4] then the distortionary costs of the overall tax system are greatly increased. The total marginal tax rate for someone in the 15 percent federal income tax bracket is more than doubled and the efficiency costs of the tax system (which go up with the square of the marginal tax rate) more than quadruple due to the payroll tax. If marginal contributions and benefits are closely linked, this can lower the effective marginal tax rate and thereby enhance economic efficiency.

The sixth principle is one of the arguments against a purely privatized system, namely that such a plan has participants—some almost certainly unknowingly—bearing too much risk about their future retirement resources. These risks can be managed by sophisticated investors, but most Social Security participants could not do so. In my view, this concern is greatly reduced or even perhaps reversed with a partially privatized plan. A two-tier system where everyone had some individual account investments would almost certainly prove a stimulus for greatly increasing the general level of financial literacy in the general population. At the same time, the tier-one benefits would provide protection from truly catastrophic financial results.

The seventh principle, that we should be aware of administrative costs, is another type of efficiency consideration. Social Security will remain the primary retirement program for the majority of Americans. It is important that their contributions not be consumed with high administrative expenses. Any privatization plan or partial privatization plan must be conscious of minimizing the administrative costs of the program. That said, the current program, which is relatively inexpensively administered, provides very poor information to participants. Annual statements are still not mailed to all participants and the statements which are sent on request are misleading. For instance, the only contributions shown on the statement are the half of payroll taxes attributed to the employee; the other half, those paid by the employer, are missing.[5] All economists agree that the employee bears both halves of the payroll tax and yet the average participant sees their projected benefits and half of their payments to the system. Any private mutual fund or insurance policy prospectus would be disallowed for failing to fully disclose the cost of the investment. In reforming the system, we should try to control administrative expenses, but clearly better and more informative communication to participants should also be a goal.

In addition to these principles, I have several observations before we examine the alternatives that have been proposed. To bring the current Social Security system into balance, revenues must be increased or benefits cut by somewhere between 25 percent and one-third. With the increased longevity already documented, most of the reform proposals advocate raising the normal retirement age (NRA) further and faster than currently legislated. Raising the normal retirement age is sometimes said to be the least painful way to cut benefits. That may be, but it should be understood that raising the normal retirement age and lowering the benefits at a given NRA are one and the same thing. There is something wrong with the analysis if one of these actions is unacceptable and the other is acceptable since economically they are identical. To make this point consider figure 1.9 where a person's primary insurance amount (the monthly benefit that they would get as a single person at age 65) is initially $800 per month. Their opportunity, set in terms of how large their monthly annuity would be at different retirement ages, is shown by the solid line in the figure. Raising the normal retirement age to 70 (so that one has to reach age 70 rather than age 65 to receive the full primary insurance amount) results in a lower opportunity set, represented in figure 1.9 by the dotted line. The opportunity set is clearly worse for the participant after the increase in the NRA and the monthly benefit is lower for all ages of retirement. The

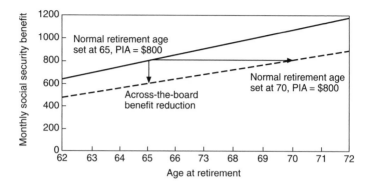

Figure 1.9
The equivalence of advancing the normal retirement age and reducing
benefits

point here, however, is that the new and reduced opportunity set is exactly the same whether it was achieved by raising the normal retirement age or by simply lowering
benefits. They are one and the same thing. It certainly can be
argued that the increased life expectancy has raised benefits
further and faster than anticipated, and that lowering them
via either mechanism (advancing the NRA or simply reducing the PIA formula) is simply an offsetting adjustment. My
observation, however, is that *raising the normal retirement age
and reducing benefits are the same thing*.

The first step in determining the retirement benefits of
participants is to calculate their average indexed monthly
earnings (AIME) over their covered work career. This is accomplished by converting the record of actual annual covered earnings into a record of indexed annual covered
earnings. Earnings from earlier years are updated by mul-
tiplying them by the ratio of today's average wage rate

in the economy to the average wage rate that prevailed when the earnings took place. The government then determines the highest thirty-five years of indexed covered annual earnings, adds them up and divides by 420 to get the AIME. People who do not have thirty-five years of covered earnings will have some zeros in the sum and thus will have a lowered AIME. People who have less than forty quarters of covered employment aren't eligible for benefits. But, for people who have more than thirty-five years of covered earnings, some of the years "don't count." For those years, there is absolutely no connection between taxes and benefits. Most reform proposals advocate increasing the number of years included in the averaging to either thirty-eight or forty years. This would almost certainly improve economic efficiency since it would improve the marginal linkage between contributions and payouts. It should be recognized, however, that this involves a cut in benefit for all participants. The indexed earnings in the newly included three or five years will be zero for some people and will be less than the already included thirty-five years by definition (the government now "counts" the best thirty-five years). So, average indexed monthly earnings will be lowered with the proposed new calculations, leading directly to lower benefits. So, the point is that *increasing the number of years in the AIME calculation involves a particular form of benefit reduction.*

My next observation is that *contributions to individual accounts are not taxes.* Several of the plans I will present here contain supplementary individual savings accounts as part of the revised Social Security program. Under most of these plans, contributions to the individual accounts are mandatory. Such contributions are not taxes, however, because the individual retains title to the funds. The funds will either be withdrawn in retirement, used to purchase a life annuity, or pass to children or designated beneficiaries if the participant does not use the money in their lifetime. The Social Security participant would have some control over how the money is invested and would receive periodic reports on how the investments are performing. The mandatory nature of the contributions and their illiquidity may make those dollars less useful than unrestricted cash, but these contributions still cannot be characterized as a tax. A tax involves an individual or household transferring resources to the central government with the individual taxpayer having essentially no say on how the money is spent. Here the participant is being forced to transfer some percentage of covered earnings to a specific account in their name and for their retirement benefits. They are taking their money out of one pocket and putting it into another. This observation that contributions to individual accounts should not be characterized as taxes gives away the secret to the plan that I mentioned in the introduction—a plan that would secure the financial solvency of the system, improve benefits, and lower taxes. By switching some of the existing contributions from OASDI to individual accounts, all of those promises can be simultaneously met.

One final observation: the Social Security system has a shorter history of success than is usually thought. The system is an intergenerational transfer plan, so the appropriate unit of time is not months or years, but generations. With this as our unit of time measurement, *the system is only three generations old* (instead of the usual measurement of sixty years). Let us date the generations as follows: generation one, those who retired in the 1940s and 1950s; generation two, those who retired in the 1960s and 1970s; and, generation three, those who retired in the 1980s or 1990s. Generation one was bound to get a great deal from Social Security. They contributed very little during their work lives and received substantial retirement benefits. From a "moneys worth" or rate-of-return point of view, they did extremely well. The second generation also benefited from significant "start-up" gains from the intergenerational transfer mechanism. During their work lives they contributed between 2.0 percent of their covered earnings (between 1937 and 1949) to 5.0 percent in 1959. In retirement, they have benefited from the much higher payroll tax rates paid by workers in the 1970s and 1980s (who contributed between 10 and 12 percent of covered earnings). Naturally, trading some percentage of your earnings for at least twice that percentage of the earnings of the next generation turns out to be a good deal. By the time we get to the third generation, the rate of return has fallen dramatically and the program is experiencing one crisis (1983) and another (1977).

Boskin, Kotlikoff, Puffert, and Shoven (1987) estimated the real rates of returns earned by different cohorts. For those born in 1915 (members of the second Social Security generation), the average real rate of return was about 5.5 percent. For those born in 1930, the real rate of return was about 3.25 percent. While their paper did not present calculations, the real rate of return for those born in the 1890s would have been much, much higher (perhaps 10 percent) although the absolute amount of gain was limited because both contributions and benefits were modest. The recent Caldwell et al. (1998) paper calculated the expected internal

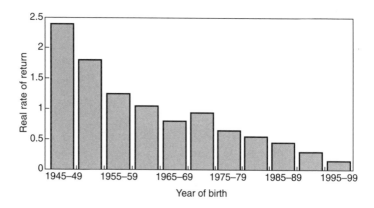

Figure 1.10
Internal rate of return by birth cohort for all OASDI benefits and contributions, as currently legislated

real rate of return for people born after World War II, using historic and currently legislated future taxes and benefits and taking into account all forms of OASDI payouts (survivor and disability benefits as well as retirement annuities). The results are shown in figure 1.10. Even without considering the benefit cuts or tax increases that are inevitable and will worsen rates of return, Caldwell et al. find that people born in the 1960s, 1970s, and 1980s face an average real rate of return declining below 1 percent and heading toward zero. My main point in all of this is that the system offered a great deal for generation one, a good deal for generation two, and at best a so-so deal for generation three, and it will almost certainly offer a substantially worse return for today's young workers. Many of them will face negative returns or at least real returns of less than 1 percent. Looked at in this generational time frame, Social Security has not worked that well since the start-up gains were exhausted.

The Alternatives

The 1994–95 Social Security Advisory Commission offered three alternative proposals for restoring the system to financial stability. One of them is called the "maintain benefits" plan and it attempts to reform the system without cutting benefits or raising taxes. The details of this proposal along with the similar menu of Social Security adjustments offered by Aaron in this volume are shown in table 1.1. The "maintain benefits" label is a bit of a misnomer; it actually cuts benefits via two of its measures. First, it raises the personal income taxes on Social Security benefits, and second, it raises the number of years that go into the calculation of the average indexed monthly earnings from thirty-five to thirty-eight years. This amounts to a decrease in benefits for all participants, although the amount of the decrease depends on the precise pattern of career earnings. The maintain benefits plan increases revenues with three measures: first, it diverts some of Medicare's revenues to OASDI; second, it raises the payroll tax rate by 1.6 percent in 2045; and third, its financial viability is based on investing 40 percent of the Trust Fund in private securities. The first of these measures appears ill advised in the extreme. How can we seriously propose saving the retirement and disability portion of Social Security by diverting revenues from the Medicare portion of the system which is in even worse financial shape? This idea certainly would not raise the Moody's rating of the financial strength of Social Security as a whole. The second idea, raising payroll taxes is not crazy on the surface, but why wait until 2045 if this is the desired approach? Why should we refuse to pay our share of the

Table 1.1
Two proposals for a single-tier Social Security tune-up

	Henry Aaron's Proposal (Alvin Hansen Lecture, Harvard, April 27, 1998)	Advisory Council's "maintain benefits" alternative
Primary insurance amount formula	No change. Spousal benefit would be cut from 50% to 33.33% of worker's benefit, however, and the benefits of surviving spouses would be raised to 75% of the couple's previous combined benefits.	No change
Inflation adjustment for benefits	Consumer Price Index less 0.5%	No change
Payroll tax rate	Immediately raise payroll tax by 0.2 percentage points on both employees and employers.	No change until 2045 when the total payroll tax rate is increased by 1.6%. Also, some revenue from the HI Trust Fund would be diverted from Medicare to OASDI beginning in 2010.
Computation period	Highest thirty-eight years of indexed earnings	Highest thirty-eight years of indexed earnings
Normal retirement age	Increase to age 67 is accelerated to 2012, then indexed to improvements in life expectancy. Gradually increase age of eligibility for early retirement from 62 to 64.	No change
Taxation of benefits	All benefits in excess of employee contributions would be fully taxable. Effectively, 85% would be taxable income.	All benefits in excess of employee contributions would be fully taxable. Effectively, 85% would be taxable income.
Coverage	All newly hired state and local employees would be covered.	All newly hired state and local employees would be covered.
Trust fund investments	"Social Security Reserve Board" would invest 40% of the Trust Fund in private common stocks.	Trust Fund would invest up to 40% of the portfolio in private stocks and bonds.

bailout of Social Security, thus leaving the bills for our grandchildren? The final idea, switching 40 percent of the Trust Fund from special issue Treasury Bonds to common stocks and corporate bonds is not fully thought through. What about the additional risks? This switch cannot produce something for nothing. If it could, the government should issue more debt and buy more private securities or we, as individuals, should borrow money and buy stocks. We all recognize that such schemes have a positive expected value but are risky in the extreme. Certainly, the Trust Fund would have a higher expected return if it invested in private securities, but it also would have an increased probability of a serious shortfall. In the event of a shortfall, who is left holding the bag?

This brings us back to the subject of the financial stability of defined-benefit retirement programs in general and the Social Security defined-benefit program in particular. Defined-benefit (DB) pension plans attempt to give workers a particular structure of benefits that "they can count on." Financing such specific promises with risky private securities works most of the time, but there always is a considerable chance of poor performance of the investments and therefore inadequate funding. If the DB pension promise has been made by a financially strong private corporation, then any shortfall in the funding would be borne by the stockholders of the corporation. In that sense, it can be said that the investment risk of the DB plan is faced by the corporation and its owners. If the corporation itself cannot make good on its promises, it is ultimately backed by the Pension Benefit Guarantee Corporation (PBGC). In effect, the taxpayers are the insurer of last resort. The point is that the investment risk is still present even when workers have a nearly iron-clad promise and it must be borne by someone—either the company's shareholders, the PBGC, or the taxpayers. That brings us to Social Security. If we were to move to a Social Security system that offers defined benefits and is partially funded with private security investments, who bears the investment risks? The answer is almost certainly the taxpayers or the workers paying payroll taxes, but the problem is that "taxpayers" and "Social Security participants" are almost the same population. The risks have hardly been shifted at all. *You cannot buy stocks and promise yourself defined benefits and think that you have somehow avoided the risks that go along with holding equities.* But that is exactly what the maintain benefit plan appears to offer. In return for investing roughly 40 percent of the OASDI Trust Fund in private securities, the advocates for this plan simply raise the assumed rate of return on the fund without any acknowledgment that someone is going to bear the extra risk involved. The point is that a universal defined benefit program, where the benefits are both defined and certain, cannot be achieved. Trying to improve the system's long-run negative balances by selling off the Treasury bonds in the Social Security Trust Fund and buying private securities is pure folly. If Moody's or Best (the organization that evaluates the financial strength of insurance companies) were to rate Social Security, does anyone think that they would be rated stronger if they sold off their government bonds and bought stocks? I doubt it. So, I believe that the Social Security Advisory Council's "maintain benefits" plan gets low marks. It simply fails to come to grips with the hard choices we face.

Henry Aaron's menu of steps shown in table 1.1 (he does not call it a plan) is better than the maintain benefits idea in several dimensions, although in my opinion it still misses the opportunity to simultaneously restore Social Security's solvency and improve national saving and economic efficiency. Aaron avoids the worst element of the maintain benefits plan, which is the transfer of funds from Medicare to OASDI. He also proposes advancing the increase in the retirement age. Like the maintain benefits plan, he increases to thirty-eight the number of years of earnings entering into the calculation of average indexed monthly earnings. Aaron would reduce the CPI-based inflation-indexation of benefits by one-half percent per year (the Boskin Commission estimates that the CPI exaggerates actual increases in the cost of living by 1.1 percent). Altogether, he reduces benefits significantly more than the maintain benefits plan. His menu includes an immediate increase in the payroll tax rate of 0.4 percent rather than the deferred 1.6 percent increase in the maintain benefits proposal. In his menu, Aaron has the Social Security Trust Fund invest in private securities, although he recognizes that this will not make retirees in general better off. The net effect of this policy will be for private pension funds to buy more government bonds and fewer corporate stocks and bonds. The private pensions will probably make the mirror-image changes to those of the Social Security Trust Fund (if not the private pension funds, who else is going to form the other side of this market?), leaving retirees in general with the same set of assets backing their retirement plans. The average rate of return realized by Social Security will be improved and the average return earned by private pension plans will be worsened, making comparisons look somewhat better for Social Security. It also could be said that private pension funds would be less risky and Social Security more risky. Is that necessarily a good thing? Rather than reconfiguring the existing pool of retirement assets, we need to increase the size of the pool. I also believe that if we are going to reduce benefits (as both the maintain benefits plan and Aaron's menu do), then we should introduce a supplementary element to the program to offset these reductions.

An alternative to trying to stabilize the finances of Social Security by trimming benefits, raising taxes, and reallocating the Trust Fund portfolio is to create a new second-tier defined-contribution component to the system. If such a system is not introduced, the temptation is to try the impossible—rescue Social Security without raising taxes or reducing benefits. With a mandatory defined-contribution plan in place, one can maintain or lower payroll taxes and cut tier-one benefits as necessary to achieve long-run financial solvency and still leave the elderly as well off as under the current system. For concreteness, consider the two double-decker or two-tier plans outlined in table 1.2. The first of them is the "individual accounts" (IA) plan of the Social Security Advisory Council, authored by Ned Gramlich, now of the Federal Reserve. The second is the 1997 plan of the Committee for Economic Development (CED). An outline of the currently legislated Social Security system is included in the table so that the proposed changes can be placed in context.

The IA plan and the CED plan have a very similar structure. In their first tier, both retain the existing defined-benefit structure, but reduce benefits to stay within the

Table 1.2
Two existing proposals for a two-tier Social Security system

	Existing Social Security	Advisory Council's Individual Accounts Plan	Committee for Economic Development
Tier One (defined benefit)			
Primary insurance amount formula	PIA = 90% of first $477 of AIME + 32% of next $2,398 + 15% of AIME > $2,875	Gradually reduce percentages of 90/22.4/10.5	Gradually reduce percentages to 90/22.4/10.5
Computation period	Highest thirty-five years of indexed earnings	Highest thirty-eight years of indexed earnings	Highest forty years of indexed earnings
Normal retirement age	65, increasing to 67 by 2023	Increase to 67 by 2011, then link NRA to improvements in longevity	Increase to 70 by 2030
Taxation of benefits	Only those with incomes above $44,000 (joint) or $34,000 (single) pay tax on 85% of benefits.	All benefits in excess of employee contributions would be fully taxable. Effectively, 85% of benefits taxable	All benefits in excess of employee contributions would be fully taxable. Effectively, 85% of benefits taxable
Spousal benefits	Spouses' PIA benefit equal to 50% to primary workers' PIA.	Gradually reduce spousal benefit from one-half to one-third	Gradually reduce spousal benefit from one-half to one-third
Coverage	State and local government employees are not required to join system.	All newly hired state and local employees would be covered.	All newly hired state and local employees would be covered.
Tier two (defined contribution)			
Contribution rate	na	1.6% of covered payroll	3.0% of covered payroll
Investment management	na	Federal government (similar to current Federal thrift savings plan)	Private sector subject to regulations on appropriate asset diversification and reasonable expenses.
Payout options	na	Mandatory annuitization	Requires that "funds are withdrawn gradually over the lifetime of the participant"

revenue constraints of the existing OASDI payroll tax rate (12.4 percent). The IA designers and the CED (and Henry Aaron) want to preserve the defined benefits for low income households as much as possible. Table 1.2 shows that with these same design guidelines, the resulting IA and CED tier-one plans turn out to be remarkably similar. This should not be surprising. If you are going to constrain the defined-benefit portion of your plan to live within a 12.4 percent payroll tax, and if you are not going to reduce benefits for those with low lifetime incomes any more than necessary, then you are likely to come out with pretty much the same answer or plan.

The first change that both the IA and CED plans make is to reduce the primary insurance amount (PIA) formula that converts average indexed monthly earnings into a monthly indexed annuity benefit for 65-year-old single participants. The benefits of all Social Security recipients are tied to their PIA. The current formula is a three-part piecewise linear formula with 90 percent of the first $477 of AIME converting to PIA and 32 percent of the next $2,398 and finally 15 percent of the AIME over $2,875. Both the IA and CED plans would preserve the 90 percent bracket, but gradually lower the conversion or slope factors in the other two brackets to 22.4 percent and 10.5 percent. Just to be clear about the magnitude of the proposed tier-one benefit reductions, consider two individuals with average indexed monthly earnings of $1,200 per month and $3,000 per month. The IA and CED plans would eventually reduce the PIA of the $1,200 per month individual from $661 per month to $591 per month, while they would reduce the PIA for the $3,000 per month individual from $1,216 to $980. The reduction for the individual with the $1,200 AIME amounts to 10.6 percent of benefits and 5.83 percent of AIME, whereas the reduction for the middle-class individual with the $3,000 AIME amounts to 19.4 percent of currently legislated benefits or 7.87 percent of AIME. In considering these and the other elements of the two proposals, remember that the IA and CED proposals also introduce a new defined-contribution tier that will provide additional retirement benefits offsetting these reductions.

The CED is more cautious than is the IA plan about living within the 12.4 percent payroll tax for its tier-one benefits. It is not clear which sets of assumptions are the more realistic, but both are responsible and reasonable. Due to their caution in assumptions, the CED proposes basing the AIME on the highest 40 years of indexed earnings (the IA plan goes only to 38 years) and the CED would gradually raise the normal retirement age to 70, whereas the IA plan would accelerate the move to 67 and then index further advances in the NRA to improvements in life expectancies. By 2030 the CED would have advanced the retirement age to 70, whereas under the IA plan the NRA would be approximately 68.5, depending on the experienced improvements in mortality.

The other features of the tier-one parts of the two plans (the IA and CED) are identical as shown in table 1.2. Both would subject 85 percent of Social Security benefits to personal income taxation, both would include all state and local workers in the system, and both would gradually reduce spousal benefits from the current 50 percent of the primary earner's PIA to one-third. Note that this cuts back the benefits of one-earner households without reducing the benefits of two-earner couples. Given the unchanged payroll tax rate and the gradually implemented cutbacks in tier-one benefits, both the IA plan and the CED plan would run a somewhat larger surplus in their tier-one program than the existing Social Security system. By the time Social Security is running a cash-flow deficit (late in the second decade of the next century), the proposed benefit cutbacks would allow these plans to still have a surplus. The tier-one parts of the IA and CED plans appear to be in balance for at least seventy-five years and possibly as perpetuities.

Where the two plans differ is in the size and details of tier two. Both set up mandatory individual defined-contribution accounts. The IA plan proposes a contribution rate of 1.6 percent, whereas the CED proposes 3.0 percent. The tier-two IA plan was designed to provide benefits that completely offset the cutbacks in the defined benefits of tier one. The CED plan would probably more than offset its tier-one cutbacks. The higher contribution rate is consistent with the general caution displayed by the CED in its economic assumptions. As was shown above, the PIA cutbacks alone amount to somewhere between zero for extremely low-wage individuals to between 5.8 and 8.0 percent of AIME for middle- and upper-middle income households. A 1.6 percent defined contribution plan can replace 6 to 7 percent of AIME even with extremely low realized real rates of return (roughly a 2.0 percent rate of return over the rate of wage inflation). A 3.0 percent defined-contribution plan would provide almost double this replacement. If returns are 4 percent or greater, then the outcomes would be much more significant. Feldstein (in the first generation Feldstein-

Samwick (1998a) proposal) has argued that 3.0 percent contributions are sufficient to replace all of the currently legislated benefits, not just fill in the gap caused by the required cutbacks to balance the system. The CED choose to be more cautious and I agree with their approach.

At this level of generalization, the IA and the CED are the same plan except that the CED version has a significantly larger second tier or program of individual accounts. Now, the devil may be in the details. The relevant details or questions here are who manages the accounts, how much choice is offered, the total expenses that they impose on the participants, and whether or not it is required that the accumulated tier-two accounts be annuitized upon retirement. The IA plan answers these issues in the following way: it proposes that the government manage the individual accounts (as with the Federal Thrift Plan for federal employees) and the accounts offered would be a small number of index funds, including a bond fund and a common stock fund. The Social Security Advisory Council assumed that the passively managed accounts of the IA plan would have a total administrative cost of 10.5 basis points or 0.105 percent of assets per year. The IA plan would require that individuals use their tier-two balances to acquire government-provided minimum guarantee inflation-indexed annuities. The CED plan differs in that it has individuals choose from an approved list of privately managed funds whose fees and level of diversification would be regulated. The CED plan would prohibit withdrawals from the individual accounts (or borrowing against them) before retirement and would also require that the funds be withdrawn gradually over the life of the participant after retirement. Although the CED stopped short of saying it explicitly, this last requirement could be met be requiring annuitization (as in the IA plan).

The administrative costs for this type of tier-two individual accounts are essentially fixed independent of the size of the account balance. The money management costs for indexed funds can be extraordinarily low (certainly under one basis point). The real costs are the bookkeeping and communications costs with employers and individual participants. The CED plan with its 3.0 percent contributions therefore has a cost advantage (or scale economy) relative to the IA plan and its 1.6 percent contribution rate. The IA choice to have the government administer that plan and limit choice to a small number of index funds was probably the correct one given the relatively small accounts that would be generated. The CED plan can afford to offer more choice and private management, but there remains the question of whether the additional choice is worth the cost. I believe that the private sector would offer high-quality competitive and appropriate products with the total administrative costs capped at 75 basis points. If this assumption is wrong, then I would have the CED plan revert to a Federal Thrift Plan type of approach.

There is much to admire in the IA/CED approach of offering both defined benefits and defined contributions. I favor the larger tier two of the CED because of its extra protection of retiree benefits and the resulting higher level of national saving. One advantage of the hybrid approach is that each tier is subject to risks, but the risks are considerably independent. The first tier is subject to the same kind of demographic and economic risks common to all unfunded defined-benefit plans. Both the IA and the CED plan propose serious cuts in benefits in the first tier to achieve long-run financial stability and the remaining tier-one benefits are fairly safe from further reductions. The participant would bear the investment risks of tier two, although the more risk averse could choose safer bond funds rather than riskier equity funds. Given the design of the plans, lower income households would have more of their benefits in the safer first tier. I like these two types of plans, but I prefer the CED plan for two closely related reasons. First, the IA second tier is almost too small for its own good. The fixed administrative costs loom larger and the increment to national saving is not enough to get excited about. The CED plan can be designed to be just like the IA plan only bigger—and in this case bigger is better.

There are two very recent entries in the two-tier plan design contest; one by Senators Moynihan and Kerry and one which I will characterize as Feldstein-Samwick II. The later designation refers to the fact that this particular plan is the second generation Feldstein-Samwick (1998b) plan (even though the first generation F-S (1997) plan, which was a complete privatization proposal, is less than two years old). The features of these late-breaking plans are outlined in table 1.3. The Moynihan plan restores Social Security to its pay-as-you-go roots. Senator Moynihan proposes lowering the payroll tax by two percentage points for the next twenty-five years and then gradually raising it as necessary to pay its defined-benefit promises. He proposes many of the same benefit cuts encountered in the IA and CED discussion. These include accelerating the increase in the normal retirement age, raising the number of years included in the AIME calculation, and increasing the personal income taxation of

Table 1.3
The Moynihan plan and the second-generation Feldstein plan

	The Moynihan plan	Feldstein-Samwick—generation II
Tier one (defined benefit)		
Primary insurance amount	No change other than lowering the indexing of the "bend points" to CPI less 1%.	No change in any of the elements of tier one, except that traditional Social Security benefits are reduced by three-fourths of the benefits taken from the second-tier individual accounts.
Inflation adjustment for benefits	CPI inflation less 1%	No change
Payroll tax rate	Lower OASDI payroll tax rate from 12.4% to 10.4% between 2000 and 2024. Gradually increase rate after 2024, reaching 12.4% in 2045 and 13.4% in 2060. Raise covered earnings cap (which is $68,400 in 1998) to $97,500 in 2003, thereafter index the cap to wage increases.	No change
Computation period	Highest thirty-eight years of indexed earnings	No change
Normal retirement age	Raise to 68 for those reaching 62 in 2017; ultimately, increase to 70 by 2065	No change
Coverage	All newly hired state and local employees would be covered.	Not specified
Earnings test	repealed	Not specified
Tier two (defined contribution)		
Contribution rate	Voluntary contribution of 2% (equaling the payroll tax cut); alternative is to receive half of the tax cut (one percent) in cash	Two-percent individual accounts are funded with cashable personal income tax credits. In the near term, these would be funded from the government surplus.
Investment management	Not specified	Regulated private investment managers
Payout options	Not specified	Mandatory annuitization

Social Security benefits. His plan reduces the indexation of benefits enjoyed by retirees to 1 percent below the official CPI, citing the Boskin Commission and the longstanding evidence that the CPI overstates increases in the cost of living. All of these elements amount to benefit cuts (relative to current legislation) cumulating to somewhere between 20 and 25 percent. With such reductions, the Moynihan plan can lower future PAYGO payroll tax rates from what their path would otherwise have been (those shown in figure 1.8). He estimates that the OASDI payroll tax rate could remain at the reduced level (10.4 percent) until 2024 and then would only gradually increase. Its level would not return to 12.4 percent until 2045 and then continue slowly climbing, reaching 13.4 percent by 2060. Moynihan's tier one (if it can be called that) is thus pretty standard stuff, a little heavy on the CPI adjustment but skipping the step of lowering the AIME to PIA conversion factors seen in the IA/CED proposals. Moynihan's tier two is novel in at least one important respect—participation is voluntary. He proposes that the 2 percent reduction in the payroll tax be split between the employer and the employee. That is, the payroll tax would be lowered by one percentage point for each. Workers would be presented with the following choice: they could either take their 1 percent cut in cash or they could ask that the employer put the entire 2 percent into an individual account. At least from the perspective of an individual worker (assuming that the wages of particular workers would not be adjusted according to their choice) the government would offer a matching deal that is almost too good to pass up.

I see at least two problems with the Moynihan plan. First, its only "almost too good to pass up." We know that firms seldom experience 401(k) participation rates above 80 or 85 percent even when they offer equally attractive matching rates (the Moynihan plan can be depicted as offering a one-for-one match). Some people will simply pass on Moynihan's tier-two offer, and the only Social Security changes that they will see are the substantial benefit reductions in the basic or tier-one part. It is quite certain that the nonparticipants in the tier-two offer will be poorer than average, less well educated than average, and younger than average. The government cannot help these nonparticipants out when they get old without completely destroying the incentives to participate in the first place. Thus, I think that this plan will hurt the poor much more than any of the other plans under discussion. Second, Moynihan's plan almost certainly involves less national saving than either the IA or CED plans that we have discussed. Remember, they cut tier-one benefits more and raise total contributions more, all of which translates into more saving.

In table 1.3, we turn to the second generation Feldstein-Samwick plan. This plan cuts the defined-benefit (or tier-one) part of the program in a novel and ingenious way. It also devotes additional funds from the general revenues of the Treasury to the Social Security system. First, it takes advantage of the fact that current and near-term projections are for a surplus in the federal government budget. Feldstein and Samwick have created a mechanism to implement President Clinton's suggestion that we devote any such surplus to shoring up the financing of Social Security. What they propose is that the government allow individuals to fund new individual Social Security accounts with 2 percent of covered payroll up to the ceiling on covered earnings (currently $68,400). The government would allow contributors to these accounts a cashable income tax credit in the amount of the contribution.[6] This makes the accounts free for everyone. Of course, the accounts are not free in a true economic sense—their cost is the opportunity cost of what else could have been done with the federal government surplus or the general revenues used to finance the cashable tax credits. Effectively, the government is placing the money into individual accounts, and one would hope that participation would be universal—if not, some automatic participation program could be devised. So far, the Feldstein-Samwick II plan has offered "free" 2 percent individual accounts, no increase in the payroll tax, and no cuts in tier-one benefits. By now, however, you must wonder about the plan—things seem too good to be true and they are. The next step is Feldstein's novel way of cutting back the defined-benefits part of the program. The payouts from the accumulated 2 percent individual accounts would take the form of supplementary or tier-two inflation indexed life annuities upon retirement. For every dollar of such benefits paid out to someone, their tier-one benefits would be reduced by $.75. The net benefit from the second tier is only $.25 on the dollar, but remember that the contributions are free from the individual's perspective. The total Social Security annuity benefits that a participant can claim are clearly more than those of the current law. One correct way to look at it is that participants are offered current benefits and one-quarter of the proceeds of free individual accounts. The government can afford to do this, the argument goes, because it is saving and investing the current and projected government surpluses in these individual accounts. This plan is very promising, I believe, in increasing saving and increasing the welfare of the elderly. Participants would be promised current benefits even if the 2 percent accounts ended up worthless (which will not happen). It is important to remember, however, that in many contexts there is a law of conservation of risks—no matter how you shuffle it, the risks have to end up somewhere. For instance, what happens if the accounts performed terribly for a generation— not likely, but not impossible—then the general taxpayers (either the payroll taxpayers or the personal income tax taxpayers) would be on the hook for undiminished benefits (the same as currently legislated) and continued contributions to the next generation's individual accounts. This does not make it a bad plan. Once the details are worked out, I believe it is very promising—just not miraculous.

There is one additional class of two-tier proposals—what could be referred to as the pure double-decker plans. Five of the twelve members of the Social Security Advisory Council support such a plan that puts more weight on individual defined contribution accounts (with 5 percent contribution rates) and less on a defined-benefit program. Table 1.4 outlines the Advisory Council's personal security accounts (PSA) plan that is sometimes referred to as the Schieber-Weaver plan after two of its proponents, Syl Schieber and Carolyn Weaver, both members of the Advisory Council. The table also presents the basics of my version of the PSA plan. I say "my version" since the version presented here avoids the tax increase that the Advisory Council version required. The PSA plan of table 1.4 is very simple. The tier-one benefits are tilted in favor of low-income individuals in the extreme—they are absolutely flat for workers with full-length thirty-five year careers. The initial tier-one benefits would be $410 per month for single retirees and $615 for married couples. People whose covered careers are less than thirty-five years would have their tier-one benefit reduced by 2 percent for each of the "missing" years. The initial, flat tier-one benefit would be indexed for real wage gains from 1998, so it would presumably grow in real value. The increase in the normal retirement age to age 67 would be accelerated to be completed by 2011, and then the NRA would be indexed to improvements in life expectancies. The age of eligibility for early retirement would also gradually be increased from its current 62 until it reached 65 by 2035.

This proposal, like all of the others, would be phased in very gradually. Only workers under the age of 55 would participate in the tier-two program. Those over 55 would get full defined benefits as currently legislated, subject only to the changes in retirement ages and benefit taxation (this program, like most of the others, subjects 85 percent of benefits to personal income taxation). Those under age 25 when the program was adopted would only get benefits under the new double-decker plan. Those between ages 25 and 55 when the program commences would get some benefits from the new program and some from the old, the fractions depending on one's year of birth.

With that very gradual transition, the program initially runs a deficit, since it has to fund all current benefits and the new 5 percent accounts and, gradually, the flat tier-one benefits as people begin to retire under the new system. The proposal is to pay for the transition both with a 1.52

Table 1.4
Two personal security account proposals

	Advisory council's personal security accounts plan	Shoven's variant of the personal security account plan
Tier one (defined benefit)		
Primary insurance amount formula	Flat $410/month for singles, $615 for couples. These figures are indexed for wage increases from 1998.	Flat $450/month for singles, $675 for couples. These figures are indexed for wage increases from 1998.
Payroll tax rate	Raised by 1.52% (to 13.92%) until 2070 when it returns to 12.4%.	No change. Remains 12.4%
Computation period	A thirty-five-year career is required for the full flat benefit. Those with a ten-year career of covered earnings receive one-half of the flat tier-one benefit. Those with more than a ten-year career get an extra 2% for each extra year, up to a total of 100%.	A thirty-five-year career is required for the full flat benefit. Those with a ten-year career of covered earnings receive one-half of the flat tier-one benefit. Those with more than a ten-year career get an extra 2% for each extra year, up to a total of 100%.
Normal retirement age	Increase to 67 by 2011, then link NRA to improvements in longevity. The age of eligibility for early retirement benefits would also be advanced gradually until reaching 65 in 2035.	Increase to 67 by 2011, then link NRA to improvements in longevity. The age of eligibility for early retirement benefits would also be advanced gradually until reaching 65 in 2035.

Taxation of benefits	Benefits taxed on a consumption tax basis meaning that 50% of benefits included in taxable income	Benefits taxed on a consumption tax basis meaning that 50% of benefits included in taxable income
Trust fund borrowing	The proposal involves a shortfall of revenues between 2000 and 2034 and a surplus thereafter. Bonds would be issued and paid off over a 75 year horizon.	The proposal involves a smaller deficit than the Advisory Council's PSA plan since it has only slightly higher tier-one benefits and 1% additional taxes plus contributions. Still initial borrowing will be paid off within 75 years.
Earnings test	Repealed	Repealed
Tier two (defined contribution)		
Contribution rate	Five percentage points of covered earnings would be rebated and paid into individual accounts.	Mandatory 2.5% contributions to PSA accounts matched by the government 1:1, bringing total contributions to 5%
Investment management	Individual directs funds to private money managers, subject to expense and appropriateness regulations	Individual directs funds to private money managers, subject to expense and appropriateness regulations.
Payout options	Flexibility without forced annuitization of tier-two account balances. Tier-one payouts would be in the form of an indexed life annuity.	Required to annuitize half of the account balance upon retirement. With the 1:1 match, this means that the assets resulting from the government contribution must be annuitized.

percentage point increase in the payroll tax rate and through borrowing. The borrowing is always substantially less than the buildup of the 5 percent accounts, so the total program actually increases saving. Eventually, the benefits from the existing Social Security program recede, allowing the Schieber-Weaver program to run a surplus, pay off the debt and even remove the 1.52 percent payroll surtax.

After the transition is over, a very simple two-part system remains that preserves the important safety-net and progressivity functions of Social Security through the tier-one "intercept." The program would increase saving from the beginning, more so as it works off the transitionary obligations. There is much to admire in the Advisory Council's PSA plan, but I think it can be improved with some relatively minor adjustments. For that reason, I have also offered my version of a PSA or double-decker plan in table 1.4.

The Advisory Council's plan appears to be a marketing nightmare—it states that they have a tax increase, when actually it decreases the payroll tax. First, it imposes an extra 1.52 percent payroll tax on workers and then it turns around and funds a 5 percent of covered earnings contribution to an individual account. Why not call this what it is, a payroll tax cut (in the Advisory Council's case to 8.92 percent) and then a mandatory 5 percent contribution to an individual account? I wanted slightly more revenue for my plan so that I could avoid the disability cuts that are part of the Advisory Council's plan and could have slightly more generous tier-one benefits. I choose to lower the payroll tax by 2.5 percentage points and then require 5 percent contributions to individual accounts. I think the best way to present my plan would be to say that we will leave the 12.4 percent OASDI tax rate in place, require a 2.5 percent contribution to individual accounts, and match that contribution with 2.5 percent from the government. All of these different ways of presenting the situation are economically equivalent. The Advisory Council does not mandate annuitization of benefits. I suggest requiring that half of the proceeds be annuitized. This would fit well with the 1:1 match presentation of the contributions, and it would protect society from concern that some people would blow all of their tier-two accumulations and then be below the poverty line with only the tier-one flat benefits. The whole package, which I have called the "Shoven variant of the PSA plan," preserves the traditional progressivity of Social Security, lowers the distortionary payroll tax, eliminates the long-term financial solvency problems of the system, and provides participants with more resources in retirement than the present system. How it does all this is simple—it forces people and society to save more.

The Choice or Choices

Now that several two-tier plans have been outlined, I will try to rank them. Before I do, however, it may be useful to consider once again the big choices—namely, staying with a pure defined-benefit plan, going to a purely privatized plan or adopting one of these hybrid DB/DC plans. The pure defined-benefit plans have several drawbacks. If they are largely unfunded, they tend to require revision after revision since the assumptions on which they are based never pan out precisely. The risks involved in a pure Social

Security DB plan are not easily quantified, but they are there. The existing DB plan suffers from a weak linkage between contributions and benefits and a low overall rate of return. Its best feature is its redistribution or "safety net" for those with low lifetime resources. I have not presented a pure privatization plan because I believe that such plans involve too much risk for participants and because it is difficult to build in the desirable income redistributions. I also think that adopting a pure DC plan involves a certain kind of time inconsistency. What would happen if we experienced a replay of the 1930s or, for that matter, our version of what's been happening in Japan for the past decade (with near zero interest rates and sharply negative rates of return on equities)? If we have abolished the DB tier-one part of Social Security, the elderly could be in bad shape in this eventuality. With their political strength, it is likely that the elderly would push for help from the government, possibly taking the form of a new PAYGO tier of benefits. Thus, the removal of the safety net is neither desirable nor politically sustainable. The better way to go is to leave the tier-one safety net (and the accompanying redistribution) in place. Any privatization plan involves important corporate governance issues (would the accounts be allowed to invest in foreign securities, tobacco companies, etc.). This issue would be massively important in a pure privatization plan as in Chile. For a host of reasons, I do not think a total privatization plan is in the cards and I do not think it should be.

The two-tier approach offers a number of important advantages. I believe that it offers the best chance for increasing national saving. It also offers significant diversification benefits. By using the first tier to redistribute resources to the poor and the second tier to reduce inefficiencies and improve the overall rate of return of system, a hybrid plan offers a "some of each" advantage. The risk efficiency advantage comes from the usual portfolio theory approach. The variability of retirement resources can be reduced because retirement income would not depend exclusively on changes in productivity and demographics (as with an unfunded DB plan) or on the performance of private financial markets (as with a pure DC plan). The two types of plans are subject to different types of risks that are far from perfectly correlated. In such a situation, the "some of each" solution offers a considerable decrease in the riskiness of retirement income over specializing in either plan.

With that preamble, here are the choices or the grades as the case may be. I believe that the two-tier plans have overwhelming advantages over the maintain benefits plan and the Aaron menu in table 1.1. So, what about the relative merits of the six hybrid plans of tables 1.2–1.4? The ranking involves judgment and all of the factors cannot be conveyed. I think we also need to work on a plan that involves the best of the best, so the final answer to reforming Social Security may take features from several of these proposals. I think that three of the six plans have the most to offer and suffer the fewest drawbacks. My personal classification is shown in table 1.5. Within categories the ranking is relatively arbitrary. The Feldstein-Samwick II plan may be the most innovative and needs further clarification and analysis. I give it a grade of "A." The CED plan is well thought

Table 1.5
Classification of alternative plans for reforming Social Security

Attractive candidates for the Social Security system of the twenty-first century	1. Shoven's variant on the PSA plan 2. CED plan 3. Feldstein-Samwick Gen II
Interesting entries, but not quite finalists	4. Advisory Council's PSA plan 5. Advisory Council's IA plan 6. Moynihan plan

through, probably involves the most new saving, and is robust, being built of conservative assumptions. Another "A." Modesty aside, I will not give myself a letter grade, partly because my plan is so clearly based on the Advisory Council's PSA plan. I took their plan and added a few tweaks. If I could just wave my hand and introduce one of these plans, this one would probably be it. I wonder, however, whether it is not a harder sell politically than either the CED plan or F-S II. The other three plans have flaws in my opinion. The official Advisory Council PSA plan is attractive; I just think the tweaks that I offered make it better. The IA plan suffers from its undersized tier-two program. Finally, the Moynihan plan is a real competitor for the "most innovative" award, but I think the voluntary nature of its tier-two is its undoing.

There you have it—I did not come down to a single best plan, but I narrowed the field considerably. In my opinion, the three first-prize hybrid plans have a great deal to offer and they are vastly superior to another round of nicks and tucks as in Greenspan 1983. That approach did not work last time and it will not work if we try it again.

Concluding Remarks

Let me conclude by emphasizing the last of the principles or goals listed earlier—namely do something as soon as possible. Politically, this is a tough problem. Social Security is popular (particularly with the elderly) and it is running a surplus. We know that it is not viable in its current form, however, and our choice is to fix it now or fix it later. If we fix it later, the problem only will be worse, much worse as figure 1.8 made clear. The vast size of the baby-boom generation is causing some of the problems facing Social Security, and they can help with the solution if we can put the new plan together within the next few years. If we fail and postpone action for another generation, we will have just transferred a massive problem to our children and grandchildren without making an honest attempt to contribute to the solution ourselves. The stakes are enormous and this is one of those cases where the right thing to do is clear. Let us announce the changes that will be made in a timely way and let us be part of the solution.

Notes

The author would like to thank Clemens Sialm for assistance and the members of the winter quarter Stanford freshman seminar for ideas and stimulation. Martin Feldstein and Sylvester Schieber kindly provided me with publications and prepublications.

1. Workers appear to be aware of the risks they face on these "defined benefits," even exaggerate them. A recent survey of young workers rated the likelihood of several events happening before they retire. Regularly scheduled passenger trips to the moon and a total cure for AIDS were judged more likely to be accomplished than continued payment of benefits by Social Security (reported in *USA Today*, April 15, 1998).

2. Most of the improvement is probably due to behavioral changes (less smoking and drinking, better diets, more prevalent use of seat belts, etc.) while only a minority of the gain can be attributed to progress in medical treatments.

3. Why saving is suboptimal is a huge topic itself. There are undoubtedly multiple reasons, including a failure of our education system to aid people in making lifecycle consumption decisions to the tax system which in some cases double and triple taxes on saving. The triple taxation argument would be that some investments are initially made with after-tax money— so the first level of tax occurs before the investment is made. With a consumption tax, that would be it. Corporate equity investments in the United States, however, face two more levels of taxation, one at the corporate level (the corporate income tax) and one at the individual level (the personal income tax on dividends and realized capital gains).

4. Since one is either eligible for Medicare benefits or not, there is zero marginal benefit from additional payments of the Medicare portion of the payroll tax.

5. The distinction between employer and employee contributions is overblown any way you look at it. In terms of who sends the money into the Treasury, all of the checks come from employers. For those not self-employed, the distinction is whether or not the payroll tax deduction shows up on the weekly or monthly paycheck (or on the annual W-2 form). Only half of the money sent to the Treasury for OASDHI is shown on these forms, with the other half hidden from workers. Whether it was hidden or not would not make any difference whatsoever if the personal income tax did not treat the "employer" and the employee contribution differently. The employee half (the half that shows up on the paycheck stub and the W-2 form) is subject to personal income taxation whereas the "employer" half is not.

6. A cashable income tax credit directly lowers one's personal income tax bill. The cashability feature means that if you do not owe as much taxes as the credit, you can still receive it in the form of a refund check from the government.

References

Aaron, Henry J. 1998. "Social Security: Tune It Up, Don't Trade It In." Paper presented at the Alvin Hansen Lecture, Harvard University, April 27.

Aaron, Henry J., B. Bosworth, and G. Burtless. 1989. *Can America Afford To Grow Old? Paying For Social Security*. Washington, D.C.: The Brookings Institution.

Boskin, Michael, L. Kotlikoff, D. Puffert, and J. Shoven. 1987. "Social Security: A Financial Appraisal Across and Within Generations." *National Tax Journal* 40: 19–34.

Caldwell, Steven, M. Favreault, A. Gantman, J. Gokhale, L. Kotlikoff, and T. Johnson. 1998. "Social Security's Treatment of Postwar Americans." Paper presented at the NBER Public Economics Meeting, Cambridge, April 16.

Committee for Economic Development. 1997. *Fixing Social Security*. New York: Committee for Economic Development.

Feldstein, Martin, and A. Samwick. 1997. "The Economics of Prefunding Social Security and Medicare Benefits." *1997 NBER Macroeconomics Annual*. Cambridge: MIT Press.

Feldstein, Martin, and A. Samwick. 1998a. "The Transition Path in Privatizing Social Security." In *Privatizing Social Security*, Martin Feldstein, ed. Chicago: University of Chicago Press.

Feldstein, Martin, and A. Samwick. 1998b. "Two Percent Personal Retirement Accounts: Their Potential Effects on Social Security Tax Rates and National Saving." NBER working paper, forthcoming.

Samuelson, Paul. 1958. "An Exact Consumption-Loan Model of Interest with and without the Social Contrivance of Money." *Journal of Political Economy* 66: 467–82.

Kotlikoff, Laurence J. and J. Sachs. 1997. "It's High Time to Privatize." *The Brookings Review* 15, no. 3 (summer): 16–22.

Moynihan, Daniel Patrick. 1998. "Social Security Saved!" Address to the Institute of Politics: Spring Exercise on Social Security Reform, John F. Kennedy School of Government, Harvard University, March 16.

Social Security Advisory Council. 1997. *Report of the 1994–96 Advisory Council on Social Security, Volume I: Findings and Recommendations*. Washington, D.C.: U.S. Government Printing Office, 484–488.

U.S. Board of Trustees of the Federal Old-Age and Survivors Insurance and Disability Insurance Trust Fund. 1997. *1997 Annual Report*. Washington, D.C.: U.S. Government Printing Office.

2 Social Security: Tune It Up, Don't Trade It In

Henry J. Aaron

Social Security has been the most successful domestic government social program of the twentieth century. It supplies income support to 44 million aged, disabled, and survivor beneficiaries. It provides the majority of income for more than half of elderly beneficiaries. Without Social Security, the incomes of half of the elderly would fall below official poverty thresholds. Social Security is, without close rival, the largest and most well-accepted instrument for extending economic assistance to low earners and large families. It lifts the incomes of 6 percent of all Americans above official poverty thresholds, more than twice as many as all government income-tested assistance in cash and in kind combined. The system is running large annual cash-flow surpluses and is projected to do so for the next two decades. It is adequately funded for the next three decades. Even if no legislative changes were made, 70 to 75 percent of benefits promised under current law could be paid indefinitely. To suggest that Social Security is in "crisis" is to engage in Orwellian doublespeak.

Social Security does, however, face a projected long-term

deficit. This deficit—equal to approximately 14 percent of average outlays—can be closed easily by modest changes in benefits or tax rates and by relaxing current restrictions on investment of trust fund reserves. Although financial considerations provide no compelling reason to modify the fundamental structure of Social Security, the passage of time along with the economic and social transformation of the United States make a careful reexamination of the major pension program in the United States desirable.

Social Security was enacted in 1935, for a nation quite different from contemporary America. The U.S. economy was wallowing in the Great Depression. Unemployment had fallen only slightly from Depression highs, approaching 25 percent of the work force, and was to remain above 10 percent for five more years. Few women worked outside the home. Almost no one, except railroad workers, had a company pension. Tax-sheltered saving, such as individual retirement accounts (IRAs), 401(k) plans, and other tax-sheltered individual retirement accounts had not been invented, for the very good reason that few people faced income taxes from which they sought shelter. Mutual funds as we know them did not exist. The average worker had not graduated from high school. Low consumption, rather than insufficient saving, was the more pressing economic problem.

In that environment, an avowedly paternalistic program like Social Security served an important and obvious need. Congress decided, for good or ill, to pay benefits to people who had contributed little and on whose behalf negligible reserves had been accumulated. Thus was born the "unfunded liability"—the excess of projected accrued benefit obligations over projected revenues—that shadows current reform discussions. Whether one agrees or disagrees with the decision made in 1939 to pay more generous benefits to workers retiring soon thereafter than past contributions warranted, history cannot be replayed. The effects of that decision are with us and we must deal with their consequences.

The transformation of U.S. economic and social life, to say nothing of the passage of more than six decades, makes a reconsideration of the structure of Social Security entirely appropriate. Should Social Security now give way, in whole or in part, to a new system that allows individuals more choice about how to invest the funds reserved to support their own retirement, disability, or survivor benefits? To be more specific, should the United States retain as its core program of income support for the retired, disabled, and survivors a *defined-benefit* pension program, that provides *disproportionate benefits to low earners* without an income or means test and to other beneficiaries thought to deserve social assistance, and that restricts these benefits to *fully indexed annuities*? Or should the United States replace the current system with a defined-contribution pension plan, in whole or in part? The question, one should be clear, is *not* whether saving in defined contribution plans and other private individual accounts is desirable. The question is whether the core program of income protection, instituted and still justified to assure an adequate income after retirement disability, or death of an earner, should retain the shape and structure of Social Security or be converted, in whole or in part, to a defined contribution plan.

Here are my answers to these questions:

• Retention of a defined-benefit structure, with mandatory annuitization and full indexation is essential for the nation's core pension program.

• Continuation of the income redistribution now effected by Social Security is highly desirable; carrying out that redistribution within a broad pension program serving all workers has important economic and political advantages that it would be rash to abandon.

• A number of modifications in Social Security would improve its ability to meet the needs of beneficiaries in the coming decades and are necessary to restore projected long-term financial balance.

• Reserve accumulation should be increased, a direction in which Congress first moved in 1977 and more definitively in 1983; these reserves should be invested according to rules similar to those governing private pensions. If these steps are taken, workers, on the average, will receive better returns on their payroll tax contributions and with less risk under Social Security than they would under any private account plan.

I begin by showing why Social Security is superior to a defined-contribution private pension accounts as the bottom tier of income protection for retirees, the disabled, and survivors. I then describe briefly the financial situation confronting Social Security. I next outline a menu of reforms to the current system that are more than sufficient to close the projected long-term deficit, without major change in the structure of Social Security. If adopted, these changes would greatly boost reserve accumulation. I then describe institutional reforms in the management of Social Security that

would permit its reserves to be invested in a fashion similar
to that of most private pensions. I conclude by showing that
reserve accumulation can do at least as much to boost U.S.
national saving as would equal deposits in personal retirement accounts.

What Should Be the Form of the Core Pension Program?

To the best of my knowledge, no one has publicly proposed
to abandon mandatory saving to support the basic pension
benefit for retirees, the disabled, and survivors. Although
some libertarian advocates of pension reform may believe that the government should not compel saving, they
understand that such a position has no political appeal
whatsoever. Participants in the Social Security debate
overwhelmingly understand that reneging on accrued enti-
tlements of the retired and active workers is politically le-
thal. Most also recognize that some form of compulsion is
necessary to overcome the widespread myopia that leads
people to save too little for distant events.

Two corollaries follow from these positions. First, rates
of return calculated for any proposed alternative to Social
Security are misleading at best, and dishonest at worst, if
they ignore the taxes required to fulfill commitments to continue paying benefits under the current system. Specifically,
to claim that a new system moving toward individual accounts would yield the rates of return of private securities
is simply wrong. The actual rate of return under any new
system is a weighted average of two yields: the gross yield
on private investments less administrative costs, and zero,
the return to current tax payers for support of accrued

benefits paid to current and subsequent retirees. *For reasons I shall explain, the rate of return generated under a privatized system would be lower—not higher—than that available under a reformed Social Security system, quite the reverse of the claim advanced by supporters of privatization.*

The second implication is that once one acknowledges that myopia is a pervasive reality of human decision making, one should also admit that standard economic models based on the assumption of stable preferences, exponential discounting, and fully rational processing of information are poor guides to the behavioral responses to modifications in Social Security.

Defined-Benefit Versus Defined-Contribution

Social Security is a defined-benefit pension plan. Such plans link workers' pensions to their earnings and years of service. In the private sector, defined-benefit plans cover about half of all pension-eligible workers and the fraction is falling. Proposed alternatives to Social Security based on private accounts are defined-contribution plans. Defined-contribution plans set amounts that employers or their workers deposit into accounts on behalf of each worker. Private defined-contribution plans now also cover half of pension-eligible workers, but the fraction is growing rapidly.

Unexpected "pension-relevant" events affect both defined-contribution and defined-benefit plans, but the effects are quite different (see table 2.1). Under defined-contribution plans, variations in asset yields and asset prices or unexpected changes in longevity, for example, change the pension that will be paid. Under defined-benefit plans,

Table 2.1
Types of risks and who bears them under defined benefit and defined contribution pensions

Risk	Who bears the risk under	
	Defined benefit	Defined contribution
Inflation	Shared	Individual[1]
Financial return	Shared	Individual
Interest rates	Shared	Individual
Recession	Blend	Individual
Extended illness	Blend	Individual[2]
Longevity	Shared	Individual[3]

1. The individual bears the risk if he or she has invested in assets other than indexed Treasury securities, first issued in 1996.
2. The loss of pension is more than four times larger if extended illness is experienced during one's twenties than during one's fifties. Under Social Security the effect on the pension is not age-dependent.
3. The individual bears longevity risk unless he or she buys an annuity.

"pension-relevant" surprises change how much the defined-benefits will cost.

The policy question is whether the United States should retain Social Security, a pure defined-benefit plan, or replace it, in whole or in part, with a defined-contribution plan. One's response depends on a number of considerations, among which two stand out.

• Should society jointly shoulder the various risks inherent in any pension plan, and should individual workers and pensioners shoulder those risks individually?

• Should social assistance to low earners and others deemed worthy of assistance, such as large families, be provided within the basic pension scheme or should these benefits be provided separately through an identified welfare program with income or means testing?

In addition, the low U.S. saving rate raises another issue—whether it is desirable and necessary to replace Social Security to boost saving. This issue, however, is distinct from the choice between defined-benefit and defined-contribution plans, as it is possible to run either kind of system with large or small reserves.

One fact about pensions is inescapable—they represent very long-term promises. From the time workers take their first teen-age jobs until they retire, four or five decades later, payroll taxes are paid on their behalf. Retirement benefits then begin and can easily last another two or even three decades. Last come survivors benefits for widows or widowers. From start to finish, the entire sequence can last three-quarters of a century or more. When promises span so many years, risks are inescapable. But defined-benefit and defined-contribution plans distribute the risks in very different ways.

Risk under Defined-Contribution Plans

Participants in defined-contribution plans face a variety of risks. Contributions usually depend on pay level and duration of employment. Once contributions have been made, the rate of accumulation depends on interest rates, dividend payouts, and movements in asset prices. Fluctuations in all three can be large and of considerable duration. While averages over long periods of time show less variation than do year-to-year changes, the pension that a worker will ultimately be able to claim depends sensitively on the timing of contributions and even more sensitively on the timing of retirement.

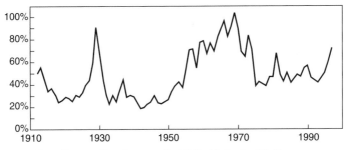

Notes: Economy-wide real wage growth = 2%; Contribution rte = 6%; 40-year career;
Invest in stocks over 40-year career; Convert to level annuity at age 62.
Prepared by Gary Burtless, The Brookings Institution.

Figure 2.1
Replacement rates of workers with forty-year careers who invest in U.S.
stock market and retire over period 1912–1997

Investment Risk   Figure 2.1 illustrates this sensitivity. It
reports simulations performed by my colleague, Gary Burtless of a simple defined-contribution pension plan. Each
year, starting in 1872 a male worker enters the labor force
at age 22 and works for forty years. Workers experience the
age earnings profile of employed men in 1995. Economy-
wide real earnings grow 2 percent a year. Each worker saves
6 percent of earnings and invests those savings in a mixture
of common stocks that yields the average dividend and capital gain of all listed securities in that year. The worker rein-
vests all dividends, which are free of individual tax when
paid. At age 62, the worker converts his accumulated savings into an annuity based on the expected mortality experience of American men in 1995 and the interest rate on
six-month commercial paper in the year when the annuity
is purchased. All insurance company fees are ignored. Figure 2.1 shows the replacement rates—the ratio of benefits

to the worker's average earnings between the ages of 54 and 58.

The dominant feature of figure 2.1 is that replacement rates vary enormously and over relatively short periods of time. The replacement rate was 104 percent for workers reaching age 62 in 1969, but 39 percent for workers turning age 62 only six years later. Pensions depend dramatically on when one buys, when one sells, and on interest rates when one purchases an annuity.

Variations of this size are a serious problem. For workers they mean that plausible expectations of retirement incomes can be abruptly undercut. Workers age 58 who looked at pensions available to 62-year-old retirees in 1969 would later suffer adverse financial conditions at a time in life when there was little they could do other than retire with much less income than they had expected or work a few years more. Workers retiring in 1975 would be still worse off if they (or Congress) looked at the handsome replacement rates made possible by the bull market of 1969 and cut back on contributions to these accounts. When 1975 rolled around and replacement rates plummeted, elected officials would be inundated with complaints about hardship among the elderly and pleas to fill in the gap. Such political concerns are not speculative, as members of Congress painfully discovered when they corrected the 1972 legislative mistake that led to excessive inflation adjustments for newly awarded Social Security benefits. To prevent this error from permanently boosting benefits, Congress had to trim the benefit formula, which it did in 1977. As a result, people reaching age 62 just after the cut back (who were christened, rather gracelessly, the "notch babies") received benefits only a few percent smaller than those awarded to people who reached age 62 just before. A national movement formed to right the "injustice" done to the notch babies. Congress stood firm, but just barely. There can be little doubt that if retirees faced the sort of benefit drops that occurred between 1969 and 1975, members of Congress would stampede to provide relief.

Workers who sought safety in bonds might have gained something in reduced price variation, although bond prices over various periods have fallen sharply in nominal terms and even more in real terms. But they would have sacrificed much in returns, as real returns on bonds have averaged less than half of those on common stocks over the long haul.

To the *intertemporal* variations in yields shown in figure 2.1 should be added even larger *interpersonal* variation in returns if workers were free to choose their portfolios. Some workers might invest in blue chip stocks, like those of Penn Central, or high yield bonds, like those of Eastern Airlines, and lose everything. Others might invest in obscure start-up companies like Microsoft and Intel and get rich. Most would fall somewhere in between. Among those who contributed identical amounts each year to their defined-contribution plans, those who had invested wisely or been lucky would be able to enjoy a comfortable retirement and generous bequests to their heirs. The less fortunate would be forced to fall back on the public dole.

Although returns would vary greatly among workers, a survey of the Employee Benefit Research Institute indicates that a larger portion of small rather than large tax-sheltered savings accounts is invested in fixed-yield assets and a smaller portion is invested in equities. Since the yield on stocks has exceeded that on bonds over most periods and low earners would tend to have relatively small accounts under a privatized system, it is likely that the average returns of low earners would be lower than those of higher earners. This pattern would reverse the Social Security policy of providing larger benefits in relation to past earnings (and taxes paid) to low earners than to high earners.

Inflation Risk   Uncertainties and risks associated with defined-contribution plans do not end when retirement begins. For pensions that are not indexed—virtually all private pensions—the effects of inflation on pensions though variable can be devastating. Inflation rates have varied widely. The purchasing power of annuities rose after issuance early in the twentieth century because prices actually fell. In recent decades inflation has eroded the purchasing power of pensions, sometimes drastically. The workers in figure 2.1 who reached age 62 in 1977 with pensions that replaced only 35 percent of earnings would have found the purchasing power of those meager pensions reduced to only 13 percent of earnings by the time they reached age 80 in 1995.

Longevity Risk   In addition to inflation risk, there is longevity risk. Unless everyone annuitizes, some will exhaust their retirement savings and end their lives impoverished. Fearing this outcome, others will needlessly deprive themselves, consume less than they could afford, and leave larger bequests than they intended.

Annuities avoids both risks, but demand for them is scant. One reason may be that the price of annuities is steep—

an average of about 20 percent of the capital sum that is annuitized.[1] Roughly half of this charge covers account management, investment management, commissions and other selling costs, and insurance company profit. The other half covers the cost of adverse selection—the terminally ill are less likely to buy annuities than are the healthy offspring of nonagenarians. Economies of scale, such as are possible in a universal mandatory system like Social Security, can drastically reduce the first cost and virtually eliminate the second.

A second reason for the unpopularity of annuities may be the myopia that prevents people from seeing the need to save when young. That same short-sightedness makes the old loathe to sacrifice current pension for protection against future inflation. The sacrifice has been considerable, as the real return on Treasury inflation-indexed securities has been running around 3.5 percent since first issued, well below returns in the rampaging bull stock market.

Risk under Social Security

Social Security benefits are not immune to risk. At the individual level, pensions depend on earnings and duration of work, as they do under defined-contribution plans. Lower-than-expected earnings or briefer-than-expected careers lower average earnings used in computing benefits. The Social Security benefit formula attenuates this risk, however, because benefits vary less than proportionately with earnings.

At the system level, a variety of economic or demographic benefits can push Social Security out of financial balance, as recent history clearly demonstrates. These events include changes in such variables as birth rates, mortality rates, labor force participation, real wage growth, and many other factors. Since Social Security is not a legally binding contract, Congress can, has, and no doubt will change the rules. When projected revenues have exceeded projected benefits, Congress has usually raised benefits. When projected revenues have fallen short of projected benefits, Congress has most often both cut benefits and raised revenues. Ordinarily, cuts in benefits for current retirees or for those soon to retire have comprised only a small part of the measures taken to close deficits, presumably because Congress is aware that most retirees and many older workers have little or no ability to adjust to benefit reductions without serious hardship.

The key point is simple: risk is inescapable. The practical question is: how should it be shared? Under a defined-contribution approach each worker/retiree must bear these risks alone. Under a defined-benefit approach like social insurance these risks are shared more broadly across society.

Level of Returns

Advocates of replacing Social Security, in whole or in part, with a defined-contribution plan claim that personal accounts would generate higher rates of return for pensioners. Even if the accounts are subject to greater risk, it is argued, the returns are so much higher that virtually everyone will come out ahead. If this argument were valid, it would constitute a very strong argument for privatization. In fact, the reverse is true. *A well-managed Social Security system will gen-*

erate higher average returns for pensioners than will personal accounts. Four factors explain why private accounts will yield lower returns, on the average, than would Social Security modified on lines I describe below.

Unfunded Liability   Whether the current system is retained or replaced, Social Security benefits must continue to be paid for many years to current retirees and older workers who will retire soon. For the first two decades or so, none of the privatization plans would materially change Social Security benefits from those promised under current law. The proposed new plans typically would not apply to workers over the age of 55 or so. Even somewhat younger workers would depend primarily on Social Security and receive meager benefits under the new systems because they had not been able to make deposits long enough to build up sizeable benefits.[2] Correct estimates of the return to workers under any alternative system must take into account the -100 percent return on taxes that young workers (those who will depend entirely on personal accounts for their own retirement benefits) must pay to cover Social Security benefits for older workers and retirees.

   This obligation—the "unfunded liability" of the Social Security system—equals the excess of the present value of benefits paid to those who have retired in the past over the present value of taxes paid on their behalf. It exists because, early in the life of Social Security, Congress decided to pay to those retirees, whose careers had been blighted by the Great Depression, benefits much larger than their payroll taxes would have justified. In subsequent years, Congress maintained and even broadened benefits.

Debates on whether those decisions were wise or foolish will, doubtlessly, occupy scholars for many years. But the practical fact is that the decisions were made and their effects are with us. Reserves that might have been accumulated were not accumulated. Contemporary and future Americans may decide to roll that liability forward to future generations, or they may decide to boost saving, gradually generating reserves that were not created earlier. If they choose the latter course, they must raise taxes on transitional generations of workers. These workers must cut their consumption to build reserves. The revenues from these taxes can be placed in individual accounts or in Social Security reserves. If invested in similar assets, the effects on active workers will be exactly the same whether Social Security is retained or replaced by personal defined-contribution accounts.[3]

Net Returns   Would the net return on private retirement accounts exceed, equal, or fall below the net returns on Social Security reserves? Under current arrangements, the answer is simple and straightforward. Social Security reserves by law must be invested in special Treasury securities with a yield equal to the average return on outstanding Treasury bonds with a maturity of four years or more. The projected annual real return on these assets is 2.8 percent. As noted above, the experience to date with individual tax-sheltered savings indicates that many savers, particularly those with small accounts would invest in conservative private securities that might well generate smaller yields than Social Security reserves do. But private retirement accounts *could* be invested in private stocks and long-term bonds, the yield on which is higher than that of Treasury securities. If they were, gross returns on private accounts would be higher than the returns Social Security *now* is projected to generate. *The reason for the differential, however, has nothing to do with privatization. It is due entirely to the restrictions governing investments of Social Security reserves.*

If these restrictions were removed and Social Security reserves were invested in passively managed index funds, the returns would exceed those earned through personal retirement accounts, whether by a little or by a lot, depends on the rules governing individual accounts. Three factors would influence the size of the advantage of Social Security over individual accounts: the limits on investment choices, their size, and rules governing annuitization.

Year after year, the large majority of actively managed funds perform more poorly than the market indices. A few astute fund managers may be able, at least for a time, to outperform market averages. But on the average, actively managed funds have performed consistently and grossly less well than have passively managed index funds. The reasons are simple and well understood. Active fund managers receive handsome salaries, in defiance of their below-index average performance. They trade too much and generate commissions and trading fees that lower net performance. And funds sold through brokers or commissioned sales staffs charge additional buying or selling fees or both. These administrative costs account for the subpar performance of actively managed funds, especially load funds. Of course, even passively managed, no-load funds spend money advertising for customers that could go to support pensions. And some funds are so small that they cannot capture economies of scale in such clerical tasks as maintaining accounts and notifying investors.

The total quantity of funds that would flow through individual retirement accounts would dwarf even the largest private portfolio. On average, these funds would not be able to generate returns before administrative expenses that differ perceptibly from market averages. The best average net return will result if these administrative costs are minimized. The way to minimize these costs is to invest funds in passively managed index funds under a regime that eliminates advertising and selling costs. Administrative arrangements are outlined below that would permit the Social Security trustees to make such investments with essentially no danger of political interference in the management of private business and with economies of scale that no private fund can match.

Unfortunately, most privatization plans do not propose to limit investment choices in this way. Experience with private mutual funds indicates that most investments would flow to actively managed accounts. The result would be a huge increase in commissions for brokerage houses, active funds managers, and insurance companies, which may explain in part the generous support some of these organizations have given to organizations expected to generate congenial results. Some simple arithmetic reveals the basis for their interest. The initial annual flow of investment funds into private accounts would range from $60 billion to $250 billion if a privatized plan were initiated in 2000. If administrative costs average the 1 percent of accumulated funds, the annual income from managing these funds would reach

$16 billion to $46 billion by 2010 after ten years and rise steadily thereafter.[4]

Although the financial industry would gain, average workers-pensioners would lose. They would lose because they would be subject to confusing and costly sales campaigns. They would lose because of costly funds management. And they would lose because the myriad plans that would inevitably seek their business, some too small to operate at efficient scale, would inevitably generate excessive clerical costs. While some other countries have licensed a small number of companies to sell retirement accounts, it is naive to believe that members of the U.S. Congress will tolerate the exclusion from "a piece of the action" of significant banks, insurance companies, brokerage houses, or mutual funds with offices in their districts or states. Thousands of organizations would fight for business and that competition would produce enormous waste, as it has done in Chile and Great Britain.[5]

In asserting that competition would be wasteful in this case, I am not alleging inefficiency in financial markets in general. Competition is wasteful in this case because the flow of funds would be so large that returns on the average could not exceed market indices (hence, active management would be a waste), because participation is mandatory to achieve a basic income guarantee (hence, sales costs are a waste), and because private annuity markets work so poorly. I shall describe below how to preserve sufficient competition necessary to assure that fund managers must meet performance standards and attend to client wants, without the needless waste that individual accounts would entail.

Annuitization   The case for mandatory annuitization is strong in a system one of whose fundamental purposes is to make sure that people do not outlive their assets. Some privatization plans would require annuitization. Presumably individuals would have to buy annuities from a private insurance company, although no plan that I am aware of has troubled to specify what the arrangements would be. If any insurance company could bid for business, one can anticipate large advertising expenditures and vigorous efforts to market to those with short life expectancies. Cancer clinics, nursing homes, and hospices would be prime sales territory. Such competitive processes are not speculative. Medicare managed-care plans focus considerable efforts and resources to enroll the healthy and disenroll the sick. They have been so successful that the Congressional Budget Office estimates that managed care has increased Medicare costs, despite the fact that managed care companies receive 5 percent less per enrollee than the average cost of similar patients served by traditional Medicare. Competition among insurance companies to achieve favorable selection among annuitants would likewise boost costs. One could avoid these costs by requiring people to buy annuities from a residual Social Security agency.

Other privatization plans permit but do not require people to annuitize. Under these plans, retirees would be given other disbursement options—to take periodic lump sums and to pass undisbursed balances to heirs through bequest. Making annuitization voluntary boosts the price of annuities, thereby discouraging purchase by some who would voluntarily buy them at prices based on average mortality and minimum clerical costs. In addition, some people will outlive any fixed withdrawal schedule, ending their lives on the dole.

None of these problems is insuperable. All could be solved or significantly reduced by government regulation of one kind or another. But the fact that they would arise and the nature of the solutions indicates why privatization, in whole or in part, would be a mistake. The wise course is to continue mandatory annuitization of defined-benefit pensions through a single public entity that can minimize clerical costs, avoid adverse selection or the temptation to spend resources to achieve favorable selection, and that reliably pays benefits for as long as beneficiaries live.

Employers' Administrative Costs   Some forms of privatization would produce huge headaches for employers. A review of current requirements under Social Security highlights what would be involved. Under current law employers are responsible for periodically transmitting payroll taxes to the Treasury Department along with personal income tax withholdings and corporation income taxes. At the end of the year, the employer provides employees with a W-2 form that lists, among other information, the total earnings covered by Social Security payroll taxes for the year. The Social Security Administration (SSA) receives a copy of the W-2 form and records covered earnings for each worker, the single piece of information that SSA requires for compiling each worker's earnings record. Social Security therefore requires virtually no additional record keeping or reporting of employers. Self-employed workers report their earnings on annual tax returns they would file even if Social

Security did not exist. Once again, the added administrative burden of Social Security is negligible.

Despite the simplicity of the process, several million errors occur annually and must be corrected. Most of these errors arise because of simple clerical mistakes, such as the transposition of digits in the Social Security number, and are easily corrected. There is ample time to make these corrections because retirement benefits are not computed until workers reach age 61.[6]

In considering the task of employers' under privatization, it is tempting to look to their current success in managing 401(k) plans. The analogy is misleading. The establishment of 401(k) plans is voluntary and most employers have not set them up. Over 60 percent of the approximately 6.5 million employers in the United States have fewer than ten employees. Only 19 percent of employees who work in firms with fewer than twenty-five employees are offered any type of retirement plan. The Employee Benefit Research Institute reports that while administrative costs excluding investment fees on private defined-contribution plans with over 10,000 participants average $49 per participant, the corresponding annual cost for plans with fifteen or fewer participants is $287.[7] In evaluating this number, keep in mind that the median annual earnings covered by Social Security in 1996 was $16,300. Under the various privatization plans, which call for allocating 2 to 6 percent of earnings to private accounts, the annual contribution for the median earner would be $326 to $978, or $13 to $38 per biweekly pay period. Furthermore, employers typically limit workers' 401k investment choices to only a few funds. If Social Security were privatized, employers would face far more formidable

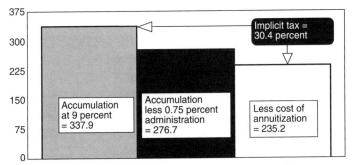

Deposit 1 per period for 40 periods; deposits grow at indicated percentage per period.

Figure 2.2
Pension accumulation, less cost of administration and annuitization

administrative problems if workers were free to select among the several thousand mutual funds, plus all banks, brokerage houses, and insurance companies. They would have to transmit checks not only for full-time, long-term workers but also for short-term and part-time workers, all of whom are now covered by Social Security. They would have to do so for new workers, some of whom would use fiduciaries with whom employers had not previously dealt. Workers would be free to change plans periodically. The typical employer would therefore have to remit small sums regularly to a very lengthy and constantly changing list of financial organizations. Even large companies would find burdensome the task of complying promptly and accurately with the requirements of such a system. Keep in mind that mutual funds now typically establish minimums on account size and acceptable deposits precisely to avoid the small deposits and balances that privatization would force upon them. Figures 2.2, 2.3, and 2.4 illustrate the magnitude of

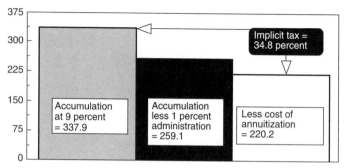

Deposit 1 per period for 40 periods; deposits grow at indicated percentage per period.

Figure 2.3
Pension accumulation, less cost of administration and annuitization

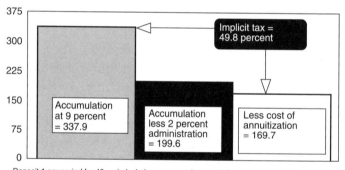

Deposit 1 per period for 40 periods; balance accumulates at indicated interest rate.

Figure 2.4
Pension accumulation, less cost of administration and annuitization

losses from needless administrative expenses. The three figures compare the accumulation over forty years of annual deposits of $1 invested in assets that yield 9 percent a year and converted costlessly into an annuity (as would be the case under Social Security) with the accumulation less administrative costs of 0.75 percent, 1.0 percent, and 2.0 percent annually and less costs of annuitization. The annuitization costs, 15 percent of the price of the annuity, consist of 10 percent for funds management, advertising and other sales costs, clerical costs, and company profits; an additional charge would be made to compensate the insurer for adverse selection—the extra costs because those who purchase annuities tend to live longer than average.

In fact, the whole process would be so cumbersome, costly, and difficult that honest mistakes would proliferate and abuses would be inevitable. Employers would be tempted to hang on to payments a few days more to earn a bit more interest. In good faith, they would send some payments to the wrong fiduciary. Some fiduciaries would charge unconscionable fees. Depositors would complain and congressional hearings would be held. One may be confident, alas, that they would be at least as colorful as those into the operations of the Internal Revenue Service.

These problems can be reduced considerably if funds are not sent initially to mutual funds and other fiduciaries, but to the SSA, which could amass the periodic deposits that employers would be sending in. When records were complete for a given year—say, around June of the following year—SSA could send lump sums, with interest, in the name of each person to the mutual fund or other fiduciary which that person has designated. This approach would reduce employer cost, but it is estimated that it would cost SSA about as much per person to handle these transactions as the current system does. In short, the most efficient privatization option would approximately double employment in the Social Security Administration!

Administrative costs could also be reduced if workers' investment choices were limited to only a few plans administered by the federal government, as is done for federal government employees under the Thrift Savings Plan. Under this arrangement employees may designate one of three passively managed plans (soon to be increased to five) that are run under contracts let by the federal government through competitive bids to a single private manager for each plan.

In summary, financial markets operate well in part because savers face financial risks in deciding how much to save and in what to invest. But the objective of social insurance is to assure retirees, the disabled, and survivors a reliable basic income. In such a system, the advantages of the risk-spreading characteristics of Social Security are of crucial importance. For this reason, the replacement of Social Security with a system of defined-contribution personal accounts would be a serious mistake. It would expose workers to risks that most are not well equipped to handle. It would raise dead-weight administrative costs and thereby lower returns to workers below what they could earn through centrally managed investments in a similar portfolio. There is something absurd in setting up a system to assure people a basic income, and then authorizing them to invest in accounts that fritter away a large part of their potential returns on needless administrative costs and that puts their basic income at jeopardy.

Why Not Partial Privatization?

Even if one acknowledges that complete replacement of Social Security with a defined-contribution plan would be unwise, one might hold that adding a defined-contribution supplement to a reduced Social Security system would be desirable. I believe that this course is unwise for three distinct and important reasons.[8]

Current Benefits Are Barely Adequate   Retaining a base income for retirees that is not sensitive to financial market fluctuations should be a central goal of national pension policy. This base consists of two elements—Social Security and defined-benefit private pensions. The private part of this protection is eroding as employers shift increasingly to defined-contribution plans. The reason for the shift is clear. Workers who plan not to remain with an employer until retirement derive little benefit from typical private defined-benefit plans, because earnings used in calculating benefits typically are not indexed for changes in prices or real wages. Furthermore, employers can avoid the financial uncertainties associated with private defined-benefit plans. Although the shift from private defined-benefit plans to private defined-contribution plans may make sense for both parties, it increases the relative importance of Social Security as a reliable source of income in retirement.

Nor are current Social Security benefits unduly generous. A recent study found that among eleven nations (most of them economically advanced) the average U.S. replacement rate at the early retirement age ranks tenth. It is less than half of those in France and the Netherlands and less than two-thirds of those in Belgium, Italy, Germany, and Spain. Furthermore, the early retirement age in all other nations is 60 (except in Italy, where it was 55), compared with age 62 in the United States.[9] I am not recommending benefit increases or reductions in the age of eligibility—quite the contrary. But comparison with benefits abroad makes it difficult to argue that Social Security benefits are especially generous. Even compared to official U.S. poverty thresholds benefits are parsimonious. Single workers employed year round always at the minimum wage who retired at age 62 received benefits in 1996 of $5,610, well under the poverty threshold of $7,525; married workers with the same wage who retired at age 62 would have received, benefits of $8,416, all below the poverty couples' poverty threshold of $9,491. Even average earners received benefits less than 1.5 times the poverty threshold if they started drawing benefits at age 65 and only 16 percent over the poverty threshold if they started benefits at age 62.

Replacing Social Security benefits, which are far from generous, even in part, with private accounts will expose retirees, most of whom have extremely modest incomes, to risks that they should not have to bear and will lower their benefits, on the average, because of increased administrative costs.

Administrative Costs, Once Again   Administrative costs, which would be bad enough under full privatization, would be proportionately larger under partial privatization. For employers, the costs of partial privatization, as noted above, could approximate annual contributions. The additional costs of funds management are quite likely to greatly exceed the estimate of 1 percent of asset value used for the full privatization option put forward by a minority on the recent Advisory Council on Social Security. Since much of administrative costs varies little with account size, the costs associated with partial privatization would be correspondingly larger (see note 4).

Disability and Survivors Insurance   Most privatization plans retain the defined-benefit structure of disability and survivors insurance, but cut benefits. Because events triggering these benefits often strike early in workers' lives, they occur well before accumulations in individual accounts could possibly support adequate pensions. Some supporters of privatization would do away with these programs and require individuals to buy disability and life insurance. This latter approach suffers from all of the shortcomings I have listed—high administrative costs, problems with annuitization, and the risk that insurers will compete for low-risk customers rather than on the basis of price and good service.

While most plans leave disability and survivor insurance in place, most also propose major benefit cuts—30 percent in several cases. These cuts in disability and survivor benefits help pay for the cost of the transition to the new system by lowering the cost of benefits under the old system. Funds from private accounts would not be available to help the disabled until they reach retirement age, and even if they were available, they would not amount to much (see note 2). Such large cuts in disability insurance benefits are hard to defend. Regrettably, advocates of privatization have not bothered to try, but have presented them without comment.

Politics of Redistribution   All large public policies that enjoy sustained political success are supported by coalitions. Housing assistance has long contained elements that appealed to the building industry and others that appeal to advocates of the poor. Farm legislation long consisted of assistance to farmers and to the indigent. Social Security has linked pensions for everyone to social assistance for low earners. In each case, people with diverse interests band together to support a program because each group understands that it is more vulnerable if it stands alone. Some purists appear to deplore this characteristic of democratic politics and would like to see each element of a program voted on separately. But political analysts understand that coalition formation is a subtle way to create weighted voting and thereby to achieve outcomes that might not be achievable if all votes were piecemeal.

Partial privatization threatens the political coalition that has enabled Social Security to sustain the nation's most far-reaching program of social assistance. Social Security provides greater assistance to the poor than do income- and means-tested cash, food, housing, and medical assistance combined. For those who attach great importance to this aspect of the Social Security program, the political implications of privatization are at the forefront.

The private accounts under most privatization plans contain no social assistance.[10] Even worse, they would be likely to provide lower returns to low earners than to high earners (because of investment patterns and fixed administrative costs). Under complete privatization, a separate program would have to be created to provide social assistance. And such programs focused on the poor have had a very mixed history in the United States.

Under partial privatization, all of the social assistance that remains would be part of a truncated Social Security system. The interest of most pensioners in the residual Social Security system would diminish. If the amount of social assistance was sustained, it would form a larger part of the shrunken program. As a result, the pension per dollar of payroll tax levied on behalf of above-average earners would necessarily fall. Resistance to continuing social assistance from above average earners would quite probably intensify. Periodic calls from above-average earners to cut back on Social Security and to move another step toward private accounts would be in the interest of high earners. Although nothing is certain, the Social Security system could easily unwind because political support would grow steadily weaker as successive changes were made.

The Projected Long-Term Deficit

Even if Social Security enjoys important advantages over defined-contribution private accounts, many who have read and listened to recent reports might doubt that it is salvageable. Media reports trumpeting enormous deficits are commonplace. Just how big is the problem?

Social Security is now running an annual cash flow surplus of over $100 billion. According to projections of both the Office of Management and Budget and the Congressional Budget Office these cash flow surpluses are projected

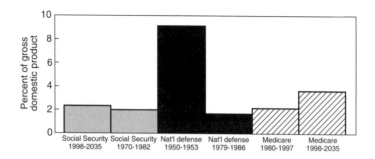

Figure 2.5
Changes in government spending (as a percentage of GDP)

to persist for two decades. As the baby boomers age, disability and retirement costs will eventually surpass revenues. Based on 1998 projections, accumulated Trust-Fund reserves can then sustain benefits until 2032. At that point, payroll tax·and other revenues are projected to be sufficient to pay approximately 75 percent of benefits promised under current law.

The increase in Social Security expenditures between 1998 and 2035, several years after the last baby boomer is retired, is projected to be approximately 2 percent of gross domestic product. While sizeable, this increase is comparable in size to other fiscal events that have not caused much notice, even though they were compressed into much briefer periods (see figure 2.5).

The most commonly cited index of the growth of the cost of Social Security, however, is not the increase in the share of GDP that the program will claim. It is, rather, the declining ratio of workers to beneficiaries—now slightly over 3 to 1 and projected to decline to 2 to 1. This projection is plausible, but misleading, for two reasons. First, workers now contributing to Social Security are paying more than is necessary to cover current benefits and administrative costs. As the number of beneficiaries increases, payroll taxes will eventually have to rise, but proportionately less than the increase in the beneficiary population.

Second, the burdens workers have to shoulder to support a dependent population depends not just on the numbers of Social Security beneficiaries but also on how many others are not working—that is, on the employment-to-population ratio. That ratio, as shown in figure 2.6, increases only slightly between 1995 and 2040. As the ratio of the elderly to the working age population rises, the number of children is projected fall and the proportion of nonworking, nonaged adults changes little. As a result, the number of mouths each worker will have to feed is projected to rise only 6 percent between 1995 and 2040.

To be sure, this ratio understates both the economic and political significance of the demographic shifts the United States will encounter. The elderly are more costly to support than are children, largely because of higher medical costs. And the shift of resources from private budgets (which bear most of the cost of supporting children) to public budgets (which bear a larger share of the costs of supporting the elderly and disabled) will pose political difficulties. But the increase in the *economic* costs of dependency are clearly modest in the aggregate. There is no crisis here either.

The fact that the total increase in the cost of Social Security is moderate and unfolds slowly, however, does not justify delay in actions to close the projected long-term deficit. While modest early actions will suffice to close the deficit,

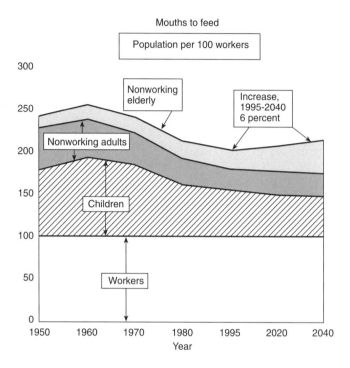

Figure 2.6
Mouths to feed (population per 100 workers)

delay would force more difficult changes later—larger benefit cuts or tax increases. Early action is desirable also because the nation will have to deal with fiscal imbalances in Medicare. The projected long-term deficit in Medicare is larger than that in Social Security. Medicare will require more fundamental changes to restore financial balance and to bring its structure in line with that of health care financing for the rest of the U.S. population. The fact that the problems of Medicare are not only larger but hit sooner could justify putting Medicare reform ahead of Social Security reform. While dealing first with Medicare might make sense, it is unlikely to happen. The Balanced Budget Act of 1997 made major changes in Medicare that will take several years to implement. Congress is not likely to return to Medicare legislation until it has had a chance to see how the 1997 legislation works out. Meanwhile, President Clinton has called the nation to debate Social Security. Social Security reform is the hand that the political system has dealt.

A Menu of Reforms

Social Security's projected long-term deficit could be closed by raising revenues an average of 16.7 percent or by cutting benefits an average 14.3 percent. Either of these changes would equalize income and outgo measured over the next seventy-five years. The menu of changes listed in table 2.2 goes further than necessary to close the projected long-term deficit. If all were adopted, they would produce a projected long-term surplus. Some of the items on the list could easily be raised; others could be lowered or dropped. The items in the menu are not necessarily the only ones or the best way to close the deficit. Rather, they show that it is not difficult to construct a reform program that entails no fundamental change in the structure of Social Security and is sufficient to close the deficit.

The size of the changes I propose grows with time. This pattern is appropriate, because Social Security is now running a sizeable cash-flow surplus, but costs rise rapidly as the baby-boom generation retires. Early steps will accelerate growth of reserves and add to national saving. Later

Table 2.2
Closing the projected long-term Social Security deficit: a menu

Item	Proportion of long-term deficit closed
1. Index benefits by 0.5 percentage points less than the CPI	33
2. Benefit cut through increasing "normal retirement age"—eliminate 12-year hiatus in increase to age 67 and index age at which unreduced benefits are paid	13
3. Increase the initial age of eligibility from 62 to 64	9
4. Cut spouses benefits from 50 percent to 33.33 percent of workers benefits and raise benefits for surviving spouses to 75 percent of the couple's combined benefit	−14
5. Increasing the averaging period from 35 to 38 years	12
6. Tax Social Security the same as private pensions	16
7. Cover all newly hired state and local employees	10
8. Raise payroll tax by 0.1 percentage points on employees and employers	16
9. Invest in diversified portfolio of government bonds, common stocks, and corporate bonds	35–45
Total	130–140

measures will prevent outlays from outstripping revenues, maintain accumulated reserves, and prevent Social Security from running deficits later on that would cut into national saving.

Reduction in Growth of Consumer Price Index (CPI)

After Social Security benefits are initially computed, they are adjusted for increases in the CPI. These adjustments assure that pensioners' benefits will retain constant purchasing power. This principle is important and just, as even small uncompensated erosion of purchasing power could seriously erode the purchasing power of benefits. A person who became disabled at age 30 would suffer a 30 percent benefit reduction by age 65 if benefits were increased by even 1 percent annually less than the increase in the cost of living.

In recent years, however, critics have concluded that the CPI overstates inflation. Estimates of the overstatement vary widely. The Bureau of Labor Statistics (BLS) has tried strenuously to incorporate estimates of quality improvements and to make other changes to counter possible biases. The weight of informed opinion holds that the corrected index still rises faster than it should; by exactly how much is in dispute. I assume that further modifications in the CPI will trim an additional 0.5 percent annually from its growth. Corrections in the CPI of this size would reduce the projected long-term deficit by as much as 33 percent. If the BLS makes the larger adjustments that some people think desirable and feasible, the contribution to closing the projected long-term deficit would be even larger.

The "Normal Retirement" Age, the Age of Initial Eligibility, and Survivors Benefits

Social Security benefits were initially first payable at age 65 and only if workers had negligible earnings. Congress later authorized payment of benefits as early as age 62, but benefits were reduced up to 20 percent. In 1983 Congress enacted a gradual increase, from 65 to 67, the age at which *unreduced* benefits are first paid. Congress delayed implementation of the change until 2000 and spread it over the succeeding twenty-two years. When fully in effect, age 65 retirees will receive benefits about 13 percent smaller than they would have received under the old law. As a byproduct of this change, the reduction for claiming benefits at age 62, the earliest age at which retirement benefits are paid, will be increased from 20 percent to 30 percent.

I propose implementing the already scheduled increase in the age at which unreduced benefits are paid ten years faster than the 1983 legislation calls for and continuing to increase it in proportion to growth of life expectancy. This change would shave 13 percent from the projected long-term deficit.

I propose two other changes in conjunction with the increase in the age at which unreduced benefits are paid. Both are intended to ameliorate the worst poverty problem among the elderly—the high poverty rate among widows and widowers.

Under current law, married couples receive two benefits. The higher earner receives a retirement pension. The lesser earner receives either a spouses pension—half of the primary earner's retirement pension—or a retirement pension if it is greater than the spouses pension. When one member of the couple dies, benefits are cut at least one-third (if a spouse's benefit is paid) and may be cut as much as half (if both members of the couple receive equal retirement benefits). The frequency and importance of the spouses benefits is diminishing as women increasingly have extended careers of their own in the paid labor force. A reduction in the spouse's benefit from one-half to one-third of the primary earner's benefit would further restrict its use. Combining this cut with a provision that survivors benefits equal to three-quarters of the couples' combined benefits would at least maintain benefits for all survivors and would increase benefits for survivors of any couple in which both workers receive a retirement benefit based on his or her own earnings. This change would cut benefits 11 percent for the diminishing number of single-earner couples—few of whom have very low incomes (the poverty rate among aged couples was 4.4 percent in 1996)—but it would increase benefits for surviving widows and widowers (among whom poverty rates were 14 percent and 23.3 percent, respectively). And it would raise costs by 14 percent of the projected long-term deficit.

The second change would be an increase in the age of initial entitlement from age 62 to age 64 (and gradually higher as the age at which unreduced benefits are paid rises above 67). This change would reduce the projected long-term deficit by about 9 percent. Benefits paid to early retirees are reduced by approximately the actuarially correct amount on the average. No retirement benefits are paid, however, to those who die between age 62 and 65. Most of any savings should probably go to liberalize access to disability benefits for those workers aged 62 to 64 who suffer from impairments that fall short of being "permanent and total," the current definition of eligibility for disability insurance. The increase is justified for a paternalistic reason—to forestall workers from claiming the increasingly discounted benefits that would be paid to retirees at age 62 or 63. Workers who elect to accept such reduced benefits consign their widows or themselves to depressed incomes when one has died and other assets have been depleted.

Averaging Period

Benefits are now based on the thirty-five years of highest adjusted earnings. Since most people work more than thirty-five years, counting more years would cause benefits to reflect average career earnings more accurately than they now do. But lengthening the averaging period also lowers benefits because earnings for currently excluded years are necessarily lower than the thirty-five highest years now used in computing benefits. The case for counting more years becomes stronger as the age of initial entitlement rises. Averaging over thirty-eight, rather than the thirty-five, years would reduce the projected long-term deficit by 12 percent. Extending the averaging period to forty years would close 20 percent of the gap. These cuts are modest in size, as indicated by the fact that a 5 percent across-the-board benefit cut, phased in over thirty years, reduces the projected long-term deficit by 21 percent.

Income Taxation of Social Security Benefits

Half a century ago, the Internal Revenue Service lost its mind and ruled that Social Security benefits were a "gratuity" that was exempt from the income tax. Tax lawyers and economists almost universally ridiculed this ruling. The Treasury Department, nevertheless, decided to wait until Congress spoke on the issue. It was a long wait. Not until 1983 did Congress pass legislation that subjected Social Security benefits to income tax. Even then, it limited the tax to half of benefits and only for couples and individuals with incomes over $32,000 and $25,000, respectively. In 1990,

Congress raised the portion of benefits subject to income tax to 85 percent, but only to the extent that incomes exceeded $34,000 for individuals and $44,000 for couples. Even now, however, the tax system treats Social Security benefits more favorably than it does private pensions.

The general pension tax rule is straightforward. The part of a pension that returns contributions on which personal income tax has already been paid is exempt from further taxation. Applying this rule to Social Security benefits would close 16 percent of the projected long-term Social Security deficit if the $25,000–$32,000 exemptions were repealed and 6 percent if they were retained.

Crediting revenue from this tax to Social Security is an anomaly. Revenues from taxing other income sources are general revenues, but those attributable to taxing Social Security benefits are earmarked for the Social Security and Medicare Trust Funds. This back-door allocation of general revenues to Social Security is partial compensation for current and past restrictions on investment of Social Security reserves that has depressed attainable yields.

Extending Coverage

Employees of states and localities have never been required to participate in Social Security, although most have joined voluntarily. Legal experts, who initially doubted whether the Constitution permitted the federal government to force state and local government participation, now mostly agree that the federal government can do so. About one-fourth of state and local government employees remain outside Social Security. Most are covered by pension plans that provide benefits similar to what a worker would obtain from Social Security or a defined-benefit private employer pension plan.

Extending Social Security coverage to all state and local workers is desirable in part because most of them work in employment covered by Social Security before, during, or after their service as state government employees, or are the spouse of a covered worker and most uncovered state and local workers eventually become eligible for benefits. Covering them throughout their working careers would extend survivors benefits to their spouses and provide inflation-proof pension coverage based on career earnings. Bringing into Social Security all newly hired workers in states and localities now outside the system would reduce the projected long-term deficit by 10 percent.

Tax Increases

Raising taxes in the United States is never popular, but seldom less so than it is now. Nevertheless, payroll tax increases might be regarded as an acceptable component of a balanced program that also included benefit reductions and restored projected long-term fiscal solvency. Increasing the payroll tax levied on employees and employers by 0.1 percentage points each, from 6.2 to 6.3 percent, would close 8 percent of the projected long-term deficit if implemented immediately. Larger tax increases have proportionately larger deficit-reduction effects. I propose an immediate increase in the payroll tax of 0.2 percentage points each on workers and employers. This change would close approximately 16 percent of the projected long-term deficit.

Investment of Reserves

From its inception, Social Security reserves could be invested only in securities guaranteed as to principle and interest by the U.S. government. In fact, nearly all reserves are invested in special issues held only by the Trust Funds. Congress thereby eliminated the possibility that public trades by the Trust Funds might be *seen* as depressing prices of government bonds and thereby causing losses to private investors. The special issues held by the Trust Funds have an additional feature not available on publicly held notes and bonds—they can be sold back to the Treasury at par at any time. This feature protects Social Security from capital losses (and denies it capital gains) if bonds must be redeemed ahead of maturity.

The limitation of Trust Fund investments to government bonds did not matter much as long as Congress financed Social Security on a "pay-as-you-go" basis. When Trust Fund balances were small, investment policy was unimportant. The limits took on increased significance after Congress adopted in 1977, and reaffirmed in 1983, a policy of "partial reserve financing" that entailed accumulation of sizeable reserves. Reserves at the end of fiscal year 1998 will exceed $700 billion, nearly twice annual benefits. By 2008, these reserves are projected to grow to roughly 3.5 times annual benefits in 2014 and reach a maximum size of $3.8 trillion in 2020. If benefits are cut or revenues are increased to restore long-term financial balance, the Trust Funds will grow considerably larger. Under these conditions investment restrictions are extremely burdensome.

The prohibition on investment of Social Security reserves in private securities has two related effects. It denies the Trust Funds and, through them, Social Security beneficiaries the full returns any prudent private pension fund manager would be expected to achieve. It also denies to Social Security beneficiaries the social returns resulting from Trust Fund accumulation which adds to national saving. These returns for the nation are equal to the average return on *private* investment, about 6 percent more than the rate of inflation. Investments in government bonds, however, earn only the government bond rate, which is projected to average 2.8 percent more than the rate of inflation over the next seventy-five years. Forcing Social Security to invest in low-yielding assets deprives retirees—especially, three-fifths of whom rely on Social Security for more than half of their retirement incomes—of the benefits of returns from a diversified portfolio on which most private pensioners can count. It also raises the payroll tax rate necessary to sustain any given level of benefits. Conversely, if one takes tax rates as given, investment restrictions lower the benefits those taxes can support.

The practical question is how to avoid this disadvantage—higher-than-necessary taxes or lower-than-possible benefits—that flows from denying those dependent on Social Security the returns from diversified investments.

General Revenues   The first option would be to use general revenues to compensate the Trust Fund fully for the reduced yield that investment restrictions force upon it. Congress could compensate the Trust Funds by transferring sums annually to make up the difference between the estimated total return to increased national saving and the yield on government bonds. The transfer required to make up the shortfall in 1998 when the average Trust Fund balance reached more than $700 billion would have been $23 billion.

General revenue transfers to social insurance plans are commonplace around the world. Many early U.S. supporters of Social Security long argued that one-third of revenue should come from general revenues. Nevertheless, after six decades of forswearing general revenue support for Social Security, this simplest of all ways to compensate Social Security taxpayers and beneficiaries for the restrictions placed on Trust Fund investments would be highly controversial and I do not include it in my menu.

Direct Investments in Private Securities Some policy-makers and analysts have concluded that it is time to permit Social Security to invest in private assets. In 1997, a plurality of the Advisory Council on Social Security recommended careful study of a plan to gradually invest as much as 40 percent of the Trust Fund in common stock index funds. But proposals to invest Social Security reserves in private securities have been criticized on both economic and political grounds.

The economic criticism points out that investing additions to the Trust Funds in private securities rather than government bonds would have no *direct* effect on the nation's saving or investment or on the capital stock or production. The Trust Funds would earn higher returns because they would hold assets other than relatively low-yielding government bonds, but private savers would earn somewhat lower returns because their portfolios would contain fewer common

stocks and increased quantities of government bonds—
those that the Trust Funds no longer purchased. These portfolio shifts would cause some secondary effects, possibly including a modest increase in the government's borrowing
rate. If one takes account of international capital movements, the full effects cannot be reliably forecast, given the
contradictory predictions of open-economy macroeconomic
models.

Investing Trust Fund reserves in shares would have an
important political and economic side-effect that arises from
budget accounting rules. Trust Fund purchases of common
stocks would be recorded as government expenditures.
Thus, Trust Fund surpluses would not appear as surpluses
in the unified budget to the extent that they are invested in
common stocks. For this reason, additions to Social Security
reserves would not provide cover for added expenditures
or tax cuts elsewhere in the federal budget. If the unified
budget was in balance with Social Security, it would be in
balance without Social Security. Investing in private equities
would thereby increase the likelihood that cash-flow surpluses in the Trust Funds would translate into added national saving.

The principle obstacle to Trust Fund investments in private securities has long been a political concern—the possibility that government officials might use Trust Fund
holdings to influence private business decisions. If this risk
were serious and inescapable, the idea of allowing the Trust
Funds to invest in private securities should be dismissed
and buried.

But these fears are, I am convinced, groundless for several
reasons. If Congress wants to influence private business, it

has better instruments than the Trust Funds. It can tax, regulate, or subsidize private companies to encourage or force them to engage in or desist from particular policies. Second, several government trust funds, including the Thrift Savings Plan for government workers and the pension plans of the Federal Reserve board, and the Tennessee Valley Authority now invest in private securities. Managers of these funds have not exercised any control over the companies in which they invest. They have pursued only financial objectives in selecting portfolios. A leading advocate of permitting the Trust Funds to invest in private securities is Francis X. Cavanaugh, a former Treasury official in the Reagan administration, who argued for years against this policy. Then, for his pains, he was placed in charge of the Thrift Savings Plan, the part of the federal government pension system that supervises investments of pension funds in private securities. Cavanaugh found that he could do his job free of political interference and confessed the error of his former position. Despite this experience, I believe that additional institutional safeguards should be put in place that would all but eliminate any residual chance that the Trust Funds might be used to interfere with business decisions.

The Social Security Reserve Board   Management of Social Security reserves could be placed in the hands of an independent board—the Social Security Reserve Board (SSRB)—modeled after the Federal Reserve board. The Federal Reserve system performs two politically charged tasks—controlling growth of the money supply and regulating private banks. Nonetheless, it has remained politically independent for eight decades. Federal Reserve governors are appointed by the president, confirmed by the Senate, serve staggered, fourteen-year terms, and cannot be removed for political reasons. Members of the SSRB should be appointed with similar protections. To manage Trust Fund reserves, the SSRB would be empowered only to select fund managers on the basis of competitive bids. The fund managers would be authorized only to make passive investments in securities—bonds or stocks—of companies chosen to represent broad market indexes. Contracts would be periodically rebid and contracts relet, based on management cost and customer service. This process would serve to maintain a measure of competition among fund managers on what counts—service to clients and cost-effective management.

To prevent the SSRB or its fund managers from exercising any voice in management of private companies and to prevent SSRB share ownership from diluting control of private shareholders, Congress could take either of two steps. It could eliminate voting rights on shares held by the SSRB. Or it could employ a number of fund managers each of whom would vote shares exclusively in the economic interest of shareholders, but none of whom would have large enough portfolios to dictate business decisions.

This system would triply insulate fund management from political control by elected officials. Long-term appointments and security of tenure would protect the SSRB from political interference. Limitation of investments to passively managed funds would prevent the SSRB from exercising power by selecting shares. The elimination of voting rights or their diffusion among independent fund mangers would prevent the SSRB from using voting power to influence company management and would protect voting rights of private shareholders from dilution. Congress and the president would have no effective way to influence private companies through the Trust Fund unless they revamped the SSRB structure. While nothing other than a constitutional amendment can prevent Congress from repealing a previously enacted law, the political costs of doing so would be high.

As a further safeguard, Congress should require the SSRB to evaluate proposed changes in Social Security benefits or taxes on the basis of defined actuarial standards. The Senate should adopt a rule requiring a super-majority vote to approve any change in Social Security that the SSRB estimates would worsen the system's long-run fiscal position. While no similar restraint is possible in the House of Representatives, because a majority vote determines the rules under which each piece of legislation is considered, a report from the SSRB that a proposed measure would weaken the financial soundness of Social Security would create political risks to irresponsible actions that do not now exist.

In a forthcoming guide to the Social Security reform debate, Robert Reischauer and I recommend, in addition, that the operations of Social Security, which are now officially "off-budget," should be moved out of the main budget totals reported by the Office of Management and the congressional Budget Office. Budget resolutions enacted annually to guide congressional action should exclude Social Security from aggregate totals. Administrative changes could add substance to the separation of Social Security from other operations of government. Congress has made the Social Security Administration (SSA) an independent agency, separate from the Department of Health and Human Services of which it once was a part and assigned the commissioner of Social Security a fixed four-year term. Three of the five Social Security trustees, however, continue to be members of the president's cabinet. Management responsibility for Social Security should be placed under the Social Security Reserve Board, making it a truly independent institution modeled on the Federal Reserve System.[11]

National Saving

Replacing a pay-as-you-go Social Security system with fully funded private accounts would probably boost national saving. But so would a decision to build up reserves within Social Security. Which approach would raise saving more?

The answer, alas, is a resounding "nobody knows!" To see why, one must examine the three conditions that determine how much new saving would result from a dollar added to the Social Security Trust Fund reserves versus a dollar deposited in a personal retirement account—yields, budget offsets, and private offsets.

Yields

If the choice is between contributions to personal retirement accounts and equal additions to Social Security reserves, the one that has the highest yield will grow fastest and add the most to saving. Since all of the contributions and investment returns accumulated in the two are held until paid out as pensions, the fund with the higher net return will tend to generate more saving. I have shown that if Trust Fund reserves can be invested in a broad diversified portfolio, the net return on Trust Fund reserves would tend to exceed that in individual accounts, principally because of lower administrative costs. If consumers weight accumulations in the Trust Funds no more heavily than they weight accumulations in personal accounts in deciding how much to consume, Trust Fund accumulations will tend to lead to higher saving.

Budget Offsets

Additions to Social Security reserves could cause Congress to raise spending or cut taxes on other operations of government by more than it would otherwise do. These budgetary responses would offset the tendency for additions to Social Security reserves to add to national saving. To the extent that additions to Trust Fund reserves are invested in common stocks, however, they do not boost the unified budget surplus. Furthermore, if Social Security operations are moved to an independent agency, or if Congress and the president alter budget accounting rules and political debate focuses on the budget exclusive of Social Security, the likelihood that Trust Fund surpluses will cause increased deficits (or reduced surpluses) on the rest of government operations is reduced. Nevertheless, it is possible that Congress will be more inclined to raise Social Security benefits or cut payroll taxes if large reserves accumulate.

On balance, I conclude that consistent Trust Fund surpluses will result in some added spending or lowered taxes outside Social Security but that the offset would be much less than dollar-for-dollar. And the offset can be reduced to the extent that Social Security reserves are invested in common stocks, if Social Security administration is moved to an independent quasipublic agency, and if budget accounting focuses on nonpension operations of government.

Private Offsets

Individuals might respond to accumulations in their personal retirement accounts in ways that could either add to or subtract from the extra saving represented by their contributions. Some recent research suggests that introducing private retirement accounts might advertise the virtues of saving and thereby increase what economists ponderously call *the propensity to save*. Educational programs that businesses have run to explain their 401(k) pension plans have raised saving, presumably by heightening people's awareness of the advantages of saving and by showing that repeated deposits, even small ones, can grow into significant assets over time.[12] Personal retirement accounts would educate workers on the power of compounded investment returns. Such reports together with reminders about the dangers of saving too little might teach frugality, leading workers to increase their saving outside of their personal retirement account.

While this "consciousness-raising" argument carries some force, the key issue is whether people who acquire a growing asset—in this case a personal retirement account—are more likely to raise or to lower current consumption. The bulk of economic research suggests that people with growing personal accounts will feel wealthier and raise consumption—that is, reduce saving. When asked, most people now express great skepticism that they will receive all the Social Security benefits current law promises, and many expect to receive none. If they begin to receive a periodic statement showing that their own personal retirement account balances are rising, they are likely to feel more secure about their retirement incomes. Based on this confidence, they are likely to increase consumption and reduce other nonretirement saving.

I conclude that creating private retirement accounts would *probably* reduce other saving; to what extent remains unclear. Experience with tax provisions designed to encourage people to save for retirement is worrisome. From 1971 through 1980 individuals saved an average of 3 percent of national product, apart from retirement saving and life insurance. They saved nothing in still nonexistent tax-sheltered individual accounts. Congress then created a variety of tax-sheltered saving vehicles to promote individual retirement saving. From 1986 through 1993, saving in tax-sheltered individual accounts reached 1.4 percent of national product. Unfortunately, voluntary saving, apart from retirement saving and life insurance, vanished entirely, dropping from 3 percent of national product to *net borrowing* of 0.4 percent of national product.[13] Although many factors other than the advent of tax-sheltered saving influenced private saving during this period, this shift in the form of saving suggests that many people just replaced saving in taxable accounts with the new tax-favored saving vehicles. Although the swap of personal retirement accounts for Social Security would differ from the asset shift that occurred between the 1970s and the 1986–1993 period, this episode serves as a warning: if you force people to save in one form they may cut back in another.

In summary, with equal deposits, Trust Fund accumulations would probably grow faster than individual account balances because of the differential in administrative costs. Some outside offsets could occur in both cases. One effect is clear—accumulating pension reserves can raise national saving, whether reserves are held in Social Security trust funds or personal retirement accounts. But saving might be lower if it were done through individual accounts than if it were done through Social Security.

Conclusion

Whatever its name, the core pension program for the United States should remain a defined-benefit pension program, that provides fully indexed annuities. The social assistance that Social Security provides is vitally important and should continue to be provided to retirees, the disabled, and survivors without the stigmatizing effects of income- or means-tests. Social Security faces a projected long-term deficit that should be closed promptly. Modest steps taken early will suffice to close it. While benefits now are not unduly generous, I believe that some reductions should be included as part of that deficit-elimination program. In addition, Social Security trustees should be freed of restrictions on investment that have deprived beneficiaries of returns that any private pension fund would be expected to achieve.

Proposals to replace Social Security, in whole or in part, with personal accounts are misconceived. They would expose the core incomes of beneficiaries to increased risks that most beneficiaries are not well-equipped to handle. They would generate lower returns, on average, than would an appropriately reformed Social Security system. In financial terms, an asset that is riskier and has a lower yield than is available elsewhere is definitely a bad deal. That, alas, is my verdict, on private accounts.

Notes

1. Mitchell et al. (1997).

2. The buildup in defined-contribution accounts tends to be slow. If constant sums are deposited periodically and earn an average real annual rate of return of 5 percent, the balance after twenty (ten) years will be only 24 (10) percent as large as it will be after forty years. If the deposits are a constant fraction of earnings that grow 2 percent annually in real terms and prices are rising 3 percent annually, the accumulation (again at a real return of 5 percent) after twenty (ten) years will be only 13 (3.5) percent of the accumulation after forty years.

3. Geanakoplos et al. (1998).

4. This calculation assumes contributions to financial accounts equal to payroll taxes of 2 to 6 percent, an 8 percent annual nominal yield with all funds reinvested, and management costs averaging 1 percent of funds on deposit. In fact, average annual administrative costs in the United Kingdom run 1.6 to 2 percent, depending on the size of the account.

5. The British system is marked by high costs of funds management. As cited by Diamond (1997, p. 49), the government actuary of the United Kingdom reports that administrative charges under its system of private accounts vary widely but that the charges levied by a typical provider run:

Initial charge: 8 percent of the invested rebate
Annual charge: 0.9 percent of the invested monies
Flat-rate charge: £2.50 per month

If deposits to accounts in the United Kingdom average 2 percent of median earnings covered by Social Security in the United States, annual contributions in the United Kingdom would average about £200 and administrative costs would reduce annual returns by 2 percentage points. If contributions average £500, the average reduction is 1.6 percentage points. The Chilean system uses a limited number of approved investment plans, but these plans use a huge number of sales agents. If the United States had a privatized system and the number of sales agents relative to population were the same as in Chile, the sale force would number approximately 400,000.

6. Earnings received after age 61 may change benefits. The benefit recomputation takes place a year or more after the earnings have been reported and applies retroactively. SSA sends out a single check to cover the correction retroactively and then adjusts future payments.

7. Employee Benefit Research Institute (1998).

8. The particular plan put forward by Senator Daniel Patrick Moynihan at the Kennedy School of Government, Harvard University, on March 16, 1998, suffers from serious shortcomings in addition to those listed in the text. First, it aggravates the projected long-term deficit by lowering payroll taxes, thereby requiring cuts in benefits that reach an average of 30 percent. Second, past experience indicates that few workers would take the option his plan gives to establish personal accounts. In 1995, virtually all tax filers with adjusted gross incomes of $30,000 a year had the option of making contributions to individual retirement accounts. In fact, only 3 percent did so. What these two facts mean is that for most workers, especially low earners, the Moynihan plan trades current tax cuts for a 30 percent benefit cut later on. As pointed out in the text below, current benefits are far from generous. The cut Moynihan proposes is somewhat larger than would eventually be necessary under current law if current benefits were paid for the next thirty years and then were cut back to available revenues.

9. Gruber and Wise (forthcoming, Table 1). The nations surveyed are Belgium, France, Italy, the Netherlands, the United Kingdom, Germany, Spain, Canada, the United States, Sweden, and Japan.

10. The privatization plan supported by Laurence Kotlikoff and Jeffrey Sachs is an exception. It would provide matching annual contributions to private accounts on behalf of low earners. The contributions would be funded from general revenues. Unfortunately, this *prospective* method of providing social assistance is inferior to the *retrospective* method of Social Security. Much assistance would go to people with temporarily low earnings but high life-time earnings. The current system provides social assistance based on low *life-time* average earnings and to large families. There is no way to provide extra assistance to large families using prospective matching.

11. I understand that fiscal policy depends on the magnitude of *all* taxes, transfers, and expenditures, appropriately weighted (although no one yet knows just what the right weights are). In that sense, fiscal policy depends on all operations of government, including Social Security. Few people now favor the use of fiscal policy for short-run stabilization, however. That job belongs to the Federal Reserve open market committee. The primary microeconomic influence of fiscal policy is on resource allocations. The primary macroeconomic use is to influence the U.S. national saving rate. In my view, budget accounting rules should be seen as utilitarian instruments to be constructed to help promote good public policy and informed debate, not as Platonic essences that, once discovered, should be enshrined. Since I believe that U.S. saving is now lower than optimal, I favor budget accounting rules that would help maintain Trust Fund surpluses as genuine additions to national saving and would help defend them against unneeded additional spending or tax cuts.

12. Bayer et al. (1996).

13. Engen and Gale (1996, Table 3–2). The fact that there is net borrowing does not imply the absence of nontax-sheltered saving; it means that borrowing in various forms more than offsets any such saving.

References

Bayer, Patrick J., B. Douglas Bernheim, and John Karl Scholz. 1996. "The Effects of Financial Education in the Workplace: Evidence from a Survey of Employers." NBER working paper no. 5655.

Diamond, Peter. 1997. "Macroeconomic Aspects of Social Security Reform." *Brookings Papers on Economic Activity*, no. 2, 1–66.

Employee Benefit Research Institute. 1998. "Are Individual Accounts Administratively Feasible?" Washington, D.C., mimeo.

Engen, Eric M., and William G. Gale. 1996. "The Effects of Fundamental Tax Reform on Saving." In Henry J. Aaron and William G. Gale, eds. *Economic Effects of Fundamental Tax Reform*. Washington, D.C.: The Brookings Institution.

Geanokoplos, John, Olivia Mitchell, and Steven Zeldes. 1998. "Would a Privatized Social Security System Really Have a Higher Rate of Return?" Paper presented to the tenth annual meeting of the National Academy of Social Insurance, Washington, D.C., January 29–30.

Gruber, Jonathan, and David Wise. Forthcoming. *Social Security Programs and Retirement Around the World.* Chicago: University of Chicago Press.

Mitchell, Olivia S., James M. Poterba, and Mark J. Warshawsky. 1997. "New Evidence on the Money's Worth of Individual Annuities." NBER working paper no. 6002.

3   Comments

ROBERT J. BARRO

The best part of Aaron's paper was the unabashed 1960s-style appreciation for a big social welfare program, namely Social Security. This enthusiasm was refreshing, especially because it reminded me of how I used to think about things when I was a kid. These days, however, most economists have become more excited about market-oriented policies such as privatization, flat-rate taxes, and property-rights enforcement—things that appear to encourage investment and long-term economic growth. So, while I would like to return to my youth and feel good about Social Security, I cannot do so.

Despite Aaron's assurances that the U.S. Social Security program has been a great success, especially in lowering inequality, I was not convinced. For one thing, I found no discussion of empirical evidence on the actual effects of Social Security on inequality or other interesting economic variables, whether in the U.S. time series or across countries. This kind of assessment is not just a matter of accounting, where one looks at the taxes paid and transfers received by individuals in various generations. It also involves behavioral responses to the program, including adjustments of lifetime work effort, private saving, private intergenerational transfers, and the tendency for members of different generations to live together or separately.

If one thinks about it, a pay-as-you-go Social Security retirement program is a strange idea. In the United States, we presently raise revenues equal to 6 to 7 percent of the gross domestic product to make transfers from young people to old people. The program produces nothing directly and most of the transfers are not from the rich to the poor, which is one reason why the program is so popular. Many of the transfers are between members of the same extended family. For example, my mother receives about $7,600 per year and my brother and I together pay in around $16,000 per year. It's not such a great deal, I suspect, even for my mother.

The Social Security program requires a vast amount of public finance—nearly equal in magnitude to that of the individual income tax—and thereby causes distortions of lifetime work decisions and savings plans. Countries that are much more generous than the United States with respect to public pension outlays are headed for real disasters, including payroll tax rates above 30 percent, just to finance this one kind of social welfare activity.

The U.S. Social Security program features considerable technical efficiency, including the administration of benefits and the raising of revenues through payroll taxes. These technical efficiencies seem nice, except that public programs with these characteristics tend to become too large.

It may be a bad idea for governments to have access to efficient taxes, such as value-added taxes and the Social Security payroll tax. Such access undoubtedly promotes big government.

The Social Security payroll tax is, in fact, a model of efficient public finance—a flat-rate levy on wages, complete with a zero marginal tax rate at the top. The tax is hard to evade and therefore encourages little socially wasteful effort aimed at evasion. The economic distortions are small in relation to the revenue raised (though not in absolute terms) because the average marginal tax rates are not so high and because the levy does not double-tax capital income. If we were willing to relinquish social security transfers, then we could—abstracting from insurmountable political problems—dispense not with the efficient payroll tax but rather with the cumbersome individual income tax, which raises about the same amount of revenue. From this perspective, the tax distortions that could be removed by eliminating Social Security would be enormous.

I did not care much for Aaron's argument that the U.S. Social Security program was not too big because some other countries, notably in Europe, had even larger programs. This is an old-style Euro-envy argument that was popular many years ago—the basic idea was that Europeans were more refined and smarter than Americans and, hence, their more socialistic policies were something that the United States ought to imitate. This general frame of mind has become less prevalent since the early 1980s, when the United States began to perform much better economically than most of the European countries. Many people now think that a variety of interventionist European programs were

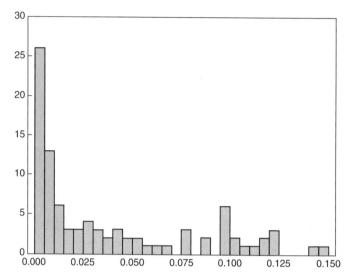

Figure 3.1
Number of countries versus ratio of public pension spending to GDP

not such good ideas, including not just overly generous public pensions but also interferences with labor markets, unrestrained disability programs, socialized medicine, and massive taxes on gasoline.

Figure 3.1 uses World Bank data to see where the United States stands in relation to other countries on the ratio of public pension outlays to GDP.[1] (The figures apply to time periods between the late 1980s and early 1990s.) The U.S. figure of 6.5 percent is well above the median value for ninety-two countries of 1.5 percent. Most of the low numbers for public pension outlays, however, are for poor countries, which tend to have small fractions of their populations in retirement ages, say at 65 and above. If one considers only twenty-four OECD countries (figure 3.2), then the United

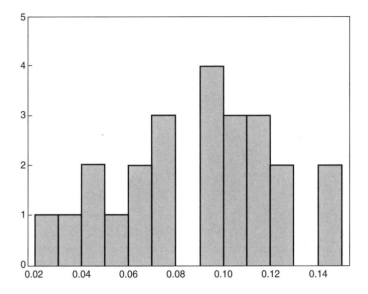

Figure 3.2
OECD countries: numbers of countries versus ratio of public pension spending to GDP

States is significantly below the median public-pension ratio of 9.8 percent.

From a regression perspective, most of the cross-country variations in the public-pension ratios can be explained by a positive effect from the proportion of the population that is aged 65 and over. There is also a significant and separate positive effect from real per capita GDP and a possible negative effect from school attainment at higher levels. The R-squared value from this regression exceeds 0.8 and the United States is very close to the regression line. Some European countries that have sharply positive residuals are Italy, Austria, Greece, Poland, and France. Other large positive residuals are for Costa Rica, Panama, Chile, and Fiji.

I agree with Aaron and Shoven that standard discussions of rates of return in pay-as-you-go and funded systems are often misguided. A funded system can offer the participants market returns, including a menu of choices to individuals about forms of assets to hold. In some contexts, a pay-as-you-go scheme can provide the representative individual with a steady-state rate of return equal to the economy's growth rate, corresponding to the growth rate of real wages and population. In most models, this growth rate falls short of real rates of return. But a full view of the rate of return also has to value the (non-steady-state) transfers given to an initial generation when a pay-as-you-go program starts up or expands. If these amounts are counted fully by subsequent generations (perhaps because they like their parents), then the overall rate of return in a pay-as-you-go system can be the same as that in a funded setup. Not surprisingly, there is a benchmark case—corresponding to an economist's vision of the absence of a free lunch—in which the programs offer identical rates of return.

I also agree with Shoven's point that no free lunch applies to shifts of Social Security reserves into riskier forms such as equities. Aaron appears to think that society can deal with the riskiness of stock returns in a pay-as-you-go system through some kind of intergenerational risk sharing, but this was not explained. In fact, one attraction of private, funded systems is that they would allow particularly risk-averse individuals to hold relatively secure assets, such as short-term treasury bills or, even better, long-term indexed government bonds.

Shoven's paper includes a description of several facts about Social Security that every sensible person is supposed

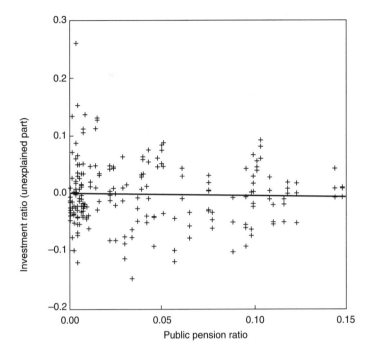

Figure 3.3
Investment ratio versus public pension spending

to believe, including that pay-as-you-go public pension programs depress the national saving rate. This relation holds
in some, but not all, theoretical models. The empirical evidence to support this hypothesis is fragile, as indicated by
the cross-country relation in figure 3.3. This figure shows
that the ratio of public pension spending to GDP (on the
horizontal axis) is virtually unrelated in a sample of approximately seventy countries to the ratio of investment to GDP
(on the vertical axis). In this construction, each country is

observed three times—for the 1960s, 1970s, and 1980s—and the influence of an array of other explanatory variables is held constant. The numbers for the investment ratio on the vertical axis measure the gap between the actual ratio and the value explained by these other variables. Basically, the public-pension ratio bears no relation to the investment ratio, which is, in turn, pretty closely related to the national saving rate.

As an aside, it is also hard to demonstrate in the cross-country data that public borrowing matters much for investment. Figure 3.4—constructed analogously to figure 3.3—shows a negligible relationship between the investment ratio and the ratio of central government public debt to GDP.

For analysts who think that pay-as-you-go Social Security has negative effects on national saving, it is worth observing that this problem likely cannot be fixed by a shift to a funded public system. Such a program implies massive accumulations of reserves with a consequent extreme political temptation to raise current benefits by spending the reserves. That is, unless a country has the discipline of Singapore, it is likely that a left-winger like Franklin Roosevelt or Richard Nixon will come along to raise benefits for the current elderly. Thus, I suggest that Shoven add to his list of things every sensible person knows the idea that it is politically infeasible to have a public program that is funded to a substantial degree. Large-scale funding appears to be sustainable only in the context of privatized (though possibly publicly mandated) Social Security.

Shoven's paper contains a useful description of alternative proposals for reforming and partially privatizing Social

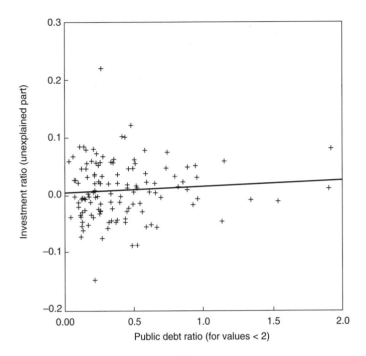

Figure 3.4
Investment ratio versus public debt

Security. I was surprised, however, that he was so favorably disposed toward the Feldstein-Samwick plan. This plan actually has little to do with Social Security and is intended mainly to absorb the prospective U.S. federal budget surplus without either raising spending, or cutting taxes, a feat that was heretofore thought to be impossible.

The key to the plan is the 75 percent offset feature on future payouts from personalized retirement accounts. The government basically gives people $1 at the outset to establish a personal account but later takes back 75 percent of each payout. The plan is economically the equivalent of giving people $.25 rather than $1, except that individuals are effectively helping the government to manage its asset portfolio (by handling the 75 percent part of the accounts). The beauty of the plan is that the $1 public contribution at the outset counts one-to-one as less federal surplus because the government's claim to future payouts (the 75 percent part) is not counted as reduced public debt. I wonder why Feldstein-Samwick did not propose a 99 percent offset.

The best reason to have a Social Security retirement system is that it can provide an income floor for old people. In this respect, Social Security is similar to other welfare programs. One special feature about Social Security is that the private resources that individuals have available during retirement depend on past saving choices, and people have the incentive to save too little if they anticipate that the government will bail them out. Hence, there is some justification for the government to mandate sufficient saving during working years so that most people will have a privately provided old-age income that exceeds the designated income floor. The size of the mandate would be set so that the typical individual would, with high probability, not require a public bailout during retirement.

Individual incentives to work, save, and incur risks are least distorted if the mandated saving flows into privately managed accounts. That is, the program should be private and funded as much as possible. There is, however, some basis for limiting the risks that an individual can incur in a pension account to reduce the chance that the individual will end up on the public dole.

A change to a private, funded program does not escape the problem of honoring commitments on pension payments to the current elderly. These promises ought to be honored, although there are questions about quantifying the degree of commitment for people who are currently below retirement age. This honoring of past promises inevitably requires taxes of some form on current and future generations. Basically, these levies should be viewed as costs created by the past mistakes of giving old people retirement benefits that greatly overmatched the present value of their payroll taxes. But these costs are basically sunk and ought not to influence decisions about a desirable form of Social Security for the future. In particular, we should start now on a transition to a system that is mainly private and funded.

Note

1. The data are from the World Bank. *Averting the Old Age Crisis* (New York: Oxford University Press, 1994), table A.5.

DAVID M. CUTLER

Depending on one's point of view, Social Security privatization is either an integral part of economic growth or a major step backward in social policy. Aaron and Shoven are more restrained than many of the authors in this literature, but their papers still reflect this difference of opinion. Shoven sees Social Security privatization as a way to shore up the retirement system for the aged. Aaron believes that privatizing Social Security will irretrievably scale back a valuable government role.

Underlying both of these views is a set of economic beliefs about what effects privatizing Social Security would have. I want to start by examining the economics of Social Security privatization and then turn to the broader debate about the management of retirement funds.

Proponents of privatization emphasize two economic benefits. First, private accounts will earn more than pay-as-you-go Social Security, so future generations will be richer if we save privately instead of through Social Security. Second, Social Security taxes and benefits will be more closely aligned under a privatized Social Security system, thus reducing labor market distortions. I discuss each of these issues in turn. I conclude that the first argument is incorrect and the second is correct but is likely small in magnitude. There is an argument for privatization based on risk spreading that I find more convincing. I turn to this last.

Privatization and Wealth Creation

Consider first the effect of Social Security privatization on national wealth. The return to private Social Security accounts would be the real interest rate, around 6 percent annually (a mix of equities and debt). As has been known since Samuelson (1958), the return to pay-as-you-go Social Security has three components: the growth of the labor force, the growth of real wages per worker, and the mortality rate between working years and retirement. Labor force growth is about 1 percent per year, as is real wage growth. Mortality rates are relatively small, so the third term is smaller. The total return to pay-as-you-go Social Security is therefore about 2 to 3 percent. Since the 6 percent private return is greater than the 2 to 3 percent public return, it is argued, future generations will be wealthier if we privatize Social Security than if we retain the pay-as-you-go system.

But this logic is entirely wrong. The reason is that it omits the financing of the government's existing Social Security obligations.

The fallacy of this argument can be illustrated with an example. Consider a world where people are young for one period and then old for one period. They pay Social Security taxes into an unfunded system when young and receive benefits when old. For convenience, suppose that labor force and real wage growth are zero, and there is no mortality between working and retirement years. Thus, people get out of the pay-as-you-go system only what they put into it. The private market return is 6 percent.

Now suppose that privatizers are elected to run the government. Recognizing the higher return in the private sector, the privatizers reduce Social Security contributions for each young person by $1 and direct that dollar to a private account. That account will earn 6 percent per year. So far, so good. But the privatization creates problems for the government budget. The government was counting on those contributions to pay out benefits to the elderly; it can no longer pay its existing obligations. One solution for the government is to borrow the amount it owes. To meet its benefit payments, the government needs to borrow an amount equal to the entire amount placed in the individual accounts—$1 from each young person.[1]

Once the government has borrowed these contributions, however, the private accounts have generated no additional national savings. The $1 saved in the accounts is offset by

$1 more of government borrowing. With no net savings, there is no increase in capital formation and thus no increase in the wealth of future generations. In future years, society will have no more income than it would have under the pay-as-you-go system.

Indeed, it can even get worse. During the next period, when the young are retired, they need to be paid the $1.06 that is the proceed of their account, but the government does not have this money. And further, since there was no increase in savings, there is no greater tax base to pay for it. For the elderly to get repaid the amount they are owed, either the young must pay more in taxes (or future young generations, if the government borrows the money again), the old must pay more in taxes (which is then refunded to them as interest payments), or Social Security benefits must be cut. If the young must pay more in taxes, they will be worse off. If the old pay more or receive fewer benefits, they will receive no net gain from privatization; what they get in a higher return on their private account is taken away in other areas. In this situation, privatization of Social Security has *distributional* consequences, but it has *no* efficiency consequences. Why is this? Future generations are richer if the nation as a whole saves more in total. Saving more through one channel, but borrowing the money through another channel, does not increase the total amount the nation saves and thus has no effect on the wealth of future generations.

There is, however, a way to privatize Social Security and make future generations better off. Consider a different privatization system. Suppose that when the young direct their contributions to private accounts, the privatizers cut Social Security benefits by $.50 per elderly person and raise taxes on the young by $.50 per person. As a result, no new borrowing is needed. The initial group of Social Security beneficiaries are worse off; their benefits have been cut. The first generation young are also worse off; although they earn $.06 more in their private account, they pay an additional $.50 in taxes. But subsequent generations are better off. They can now save their $1 in an account earning 6 percent, without having to pay more taxes to support the elderly.

The key to this example is that the tax increase and benefit cut increase national saving; they take from people who would have consumed and save it for future generations. This additional savings generates the higher rate of return. But note that private accounts are essentially irrelevant in this example. Future generations would be equally well off if the government cut Social Security benefits by $.50, raised taxes on the young by $.50, and invested the money itself. The government would earn the 6 percent return, which it could give to future young people in the same manner they would have earned it themselves.

In short, setting up private accounts for Social Security has no real effect by itself on the economy. All of the gains from Social Security privatization come from raising taxes or cutting benefits, which might then be used to increase national savings. In the Social Security privatization debate, the need for tax increases or benefit cuts to finance foregone revenues is termed the "transition problem." The wording suggests this problem is minor. In reality, transition financing is the source of all of the gains from privatization and deserves much more attention than it receives.

Indeed, rather than focus so heavily on whether we should have private accounts or not, the better question to ask is whether we should have a tax increase or cut in government spending that can be used to increase national saving. I believe that we should. Private returns are high, suggesting that we do not save enough. And the country is aging; in the next twenty years the ratio of workers to retirees will fall precipitously. A prudent society would save more to meet this coming burden.

Of course, there is no reason why this additional saving need be done through Social Security. One could just as easily raise non-Social Security taxes and cut non-Social Security spending and build up the same surplus. Since the problems of aging show up particularly acutely in old-age insurance, however, there is a reasonable argument to make for saving more through Social Security.

There are numerous opportunities for building up a surplus through Social Security; Aaron and Shoven present excellent lists. Some potential changes are good policy, like raising the normal and early retirement ages and increasing the averaging period in determining AIME. Other changes make much less sense, like cutting disability benefits. I do not want to propose one set of reforms as much as encourage more discussion about these reforms. Since these reforms are the source of all of the increase in national saving, they should be the primary focus of discussion.

If we do save more through Social Security, we need to decide who should manage the additional saving—the government or individuals through private accounts. This is a complicated question. The argument for individual accounts is that governments are rarely good at running surpluses—they are tempted to spend the money or refund it as tax credits with no salutary effects on savings.[2] The argument for government investment is that economies of scale from large investments will drive down administrative costs. In addition, many people (particularly the poor) may not be good investors. I suspect that it is better to have individual accounts than to have the government invest the money, but this issue needs more research.

On net, therefore, it makes sense to use Social Security reform to increase national saving. But Social Security privatization is not an integral part of this reform. Setting up private accounts might be beneficial—for example, in ensuring that money saved contributes to national saving—but the claim of the privatization proponents that setting up individual accounts will enable society to earn higher returns is simply incorrect.

Privatization and Labor Supply

The second potential benefit from Social Security privatization is the possibility of linking benefits and taxes at the margin, and thus reducing labor supply distortions. In pay-as-you-go Social Security, the taxes one pays into the system rarely equal the benefits one receives at the margin. For example, secondary earners pay the entire payroll tax (nearly 12 percent, including the employer and employee share) but frequently claim benefits as a spouse. As a result, they pay more when they earn more but receive no additional benefits from earning more. This discrepancy between marginal payments and marginal benefits is an implicit form of taxation, and may have adverse labor supply effects in the same fashion as explicit taxes. Individuals might respond to these taxes by distorting their hours of work, retiring sooner, reducing their effort on the job, or taking compensation in a nontax fashion.

With a system of individual accounts, contributions and benefits could be more closely linked. If people get out of the system what they put in, there is no implicit tax rate, and thus no incentive for people to distort their behavior.

The question is whether these gains are real and how large they are. There are likely to be gains from this effect, but I suspect they are small. There are two reasons for skepticism. First, the literature does not suggest that labor supply is particularly elastic for workers below the Social Security earnings maximum (about $65,000 per year; above that amount, the marginal tax rate is zero). For prime-age men, labor supply elasticities are generally estimated to be close to zero, although for women they are positive.

The second reason for skepticism is that contributions and benefits may not be linked at the margin even in a privatized Social Security system. For example, most privatization proposals suggest making additional contributions into accounts for the poor, at the expense of accounts for the rich. This redistribution would increase the progressivity of the system, but would have the same adverse efficiency consequences as does redistribution in the current system. Similarly, most proposals restrict where account balances may be invested (for example, in broad market securities) and how individuals can access the funds (for example, a certain percentage must be annuitized). Each of these restrictions reduces what individuals may perceive as the benefits of their account, thus reducing the efficiency gains from privatization. Finally, if people do not save enough on their own because they have very high discount rates, they might not perceive increased benefits in the future as a reason to work more today, even if the benefits are actuarially fair.

The net effect is that privatization is likely to increase the efficiency of the labor market, but I suspect the effects are small. Indeed, most of the estimates that have been made— even those that assume greater benefit-tax linkage from a privatized Social Security system than I suspect is possible (for example, Kotlikoff, Smetters, and Wallister, 1998)—do not find large gains from reducing labor supply distortions.

Privatization and Risk

Perhaps the most convincing rationale for privatizing a portion of Social Security has to do with risk management. Both defined-benefit and defined-contribution retirement systems have risks associated with them. The risks in a defined-contribution system are obvious. If asset returns are low, the elderly will suffer. And even if the market as a whole does well, some people may invest heavily in particular assets that do not perform well.

Defined-benefit systems are also risky, however. The growth of real wages, the labor force (largely determined by fertility rates), and mortality all change over time. This risk is particularly important because Social Security must finance retirement many years in the future.

An example illustrates the risk. Between 1950 and 1970, real wage growth in the United States averaged about 2 percent annually. Between 1970 and 1990, the growth rate was closer to 0 percent. Which of these two rates should we assume will prevail for the next seventy-five years, or should an average be used? This choice has important consequences; the actuarial status of Social Security varies dramatically with changes in real wage growth of even 0.1 percent annually.

Shoven suggests an answer to the risk issue: since both defined-benefit and defined-contribution systems are risky, we should have both types of systems. I agree with this solution. As a general matter, society appears overly invested in defined-benefit savings instruments and insufficiently invested in defined-contribution instruments. A partial privatization of Social Security is one way to even out this balance.

Summary

On net, I come out near where Shoven does. Partial privatization of Social Security is a good idea if it contributes to saving more as a society and offsets some of the risk of a defined-benefit retirement system. But perhaps more important, I find the debate about Social Security privatization inadequate. The debate is being guided by myths—society can be wealthier and no one need be hurt, privatization will raise labor supply substantially. These claims are less true than is suggested, or are completely false. Conducting a debate on this basis is dangerous. If we persist in promising people a free lunch, what will we tell them when the bill arrives?

Notes

1. The borrowing need not equal the account contribution on a person-by-person basis, but in aggregate it must be that amount.

2. Several proposals call for distributing the current budget surplus to Social Security accounts. This proposal only adds positively to the economy if the government would otherwise have spent the money and thus it would not have been saved.

References

Kotlikoff, Laurence J., Kent A. Smetters, and Jan Walliser. 1998. "Social Security: Privatization and Progressivity." NBER working paper no. 6428.

Samuelson, Paul. 1958. "An Exact Consumption—Loan Model of Interest with or without the Social Contrivance of Money." *Journal of Political Economy* 66: 467–482.

ALICIA H. MUNNELL

Although Shoven and Aaron both profess the same goals for Social Security, Aaron's proposal gets us there and Shoven's does not. The question is where—with such laudable objectives—does Shoven go wrong. In my view, he and others who propose cutting back on Social Security to make room for privatized accounts make five errors. First, they fail to consider the most serious alternative to privatized accounts—namely, a partially funded defined-benefit plan. Second, they dismiss in far too cavalier a fashion the possibility of equity investment through the Trust Funds. Third, they have a completely unrealistic notion about the predictability of benefits under a defined-contribution plan. Fourth, they make a priority of increasing efficiency but do not properly evaluate the outcome of their proposals. Fifth, they believe that changing a benefit structure from a defined-benefit plan to a defined-contribution plan can make a tax not a tax.

Privatized Account Advocates Ignore the Real
Alternative: A Partially Funded Defined-Benefit Plan

Social Security is on the national agenda because the system faces a projected long-term deficit. But things are different than they were in 1983 when Congress last acted to restore financial balance; this time the system is not facing a short-term financing crisis. In fact, government actuaries calculate that the system has an adequate flow of revenues until 2032 and can cover three-quarters of promised benefits for decades thereafter. The emergence of a long-term deficit in the absence of a short-term crisis means that policymakers can consider comprehensive reform as well as incremental fixes to the system.

In considering both incremental and comprehensive reform, two relatively new considerations are playing an important role. One is the maturation of the Social Security program. Unlike earlier generations who received large benefits relative to the taxes they paid, today's workers face a sharp decline in returns that they can expect to receive on their payroll tax contributions (the so-called money's worth issue). Since raising taxes or reducing benefits will only worsen returns, almost all reform plans involve equity investment in one form or another to provide additional revenue. The second factor influencing the Social Security reform debate is concern about our low levels of national saving. This concern, along with the desire to avoid high pay-as-you-go tax rates in the future, has spawned considerable interest in some prefunding.

Almost all the proposals that Shoven considers, with the notable exception of Senator Moynihan's plan, respond to

these concerns. Thus, the Social Security debate in this fo-
rum is not about whether to accumulate reserves through
the Social Security program to increase national saving. Both
proposals to maintain Social Security's existing defined-
benefit plan and proposals to institute individual accounts
involve a substantial accumulation of assets. Nor is the debate about whether to broaden the investment options for
Social Security participants. Everyone here agrees that those
covered by Social Security should have access to the higher
risks and higher returns associated with equity investment.
In other words, the questions of prefunding and of broaden-
ing the portfolio are not at issue.

Rather, the debate is—given prefunding and given the
desire to invest in equities—whether this is better done in
the central Social Security Trust Funds or in privatized accounts. My view is that the economics argue strongly in favor of a pooled defined-benefit approach over privatized
accounts. Thus, Shoven heads down the wrong path right
in the beginning when he omits a partially funded defined-
benefit plan from the list of proposals that he intends to
analyze.

Investing the Trust Funds in Equities Is Both Feasible and Desirable

A major reason that a partially funded defined-benefit plan
does not appear on Shoven's list is that he dismisses investing in equities through the central Trust Funds. Instead,
he advocates equity investment through a mandatory IRA-
type account. But such an approach would put much of people's basic retirement benefits at risk. Their basic benefit

would depend on their individual investment decisions. What stocks did they buy? When did they buy them? When did they sell? Uncertain outcomes may be appropriate for supplementary retirement benefits, but not for the basic guarantee. Herb Stein summarized the argument best.

If there is no social interest in the income people have at retirement, there is no justification for the Social Security tax. If there is such an interest, there is a need for policies that will assure that the intended amount of income is *always* forthcoming. It is not sufficient to say that some people who are very smart or very lucky in the management of their funds will have high incomes and those who are not will have low incomes and that everything averages out.

The IRA-type approach also creates a very real political risk that account holders would pressure Congress for access to these accounts, albeit for worthy purposes. Although proponents argue against such withdrawals, experience with existing IRAs and 401(k)s suggests that holding the line might be quite difficult. To the extent that Congress acquiesces and allows early access, retirees will end up with inadequate retirement income.

The IRA-type approach also raises troublesome questions about transforming accumulated reserves into annuities. Without such a transformation, individuals stand a good chance of outliving their savings. But few people purchase private annuities and costs are high in the private annuity market. Moreover, the private annuity market would have a hard time providing inflation-adjusted benefits.

The IRA-type approach also puts dependent spouses at risk. A defined-benefit system with auxiliary benefits is very different from a defined-contribution system where the annuity protection for the family is paid for by the worker and involves choice. The evidence suggests that left on their own, workers do not always make very good choices for themselves, much less for their dependents. The small size of the current U.S. annuity market suggests that retirees do not choose to annuitize their accumulations. Evidence from the United Kingdom suggests that people do not purchase inflation protection even when they have the opportunity. Finally, pre-ERISA data indicate that many workers select single-life annuities with no protection for surviving spouses. Thus, elderly widows, who already suffer very high rates of poverty, could be made worse off under a system of privatized accounts.

Finally, an IRA-type account would also be extremely costly. Shoven mentions 75 basis points, but that is probably on the low side. The Advisory Council estimates that an IRA-type individual account would cost 100 basis points per year. A 100-basis point annual charge sounds benign, but estimates by Peter Diamond show that it would reduce total accumulations by roughly 20 percent over a forty-year work life. That means benefits would be 20 percent lower than they would have been in the absence of the transaction costs. Moreover, while the 100-basis-point estimate includes the cost of marketing, tracking, and maintaining the account, it does not include brokerage fees. If the individual does not select an index fund, then transaction costs may be twice as high. Indeed, costs actually experienced in the United Kingdom, which has a system of individual accounts, have been considerably higher than the Advisory Council estimate. Finally, because these transaction costs involve a large flat charge per account, they will be considerably more burdensome for low-income participants than for those with higher incomes.

Shoven is not wedded to the IRA-type approach if the costs are too high; he would be happy to fall back to the 401(k) or federal Thrift Savings Plan (TSP) approach. Instead of individuals holding their funds and investing them in anything they like, the government would hold the money and designate a series of investment options. This buys us virtually nothing, however, over investing accumulated Trust-Fund reserves directly. First, the TSP approach introduces most of the same unpredictability into retirement income as the IRA-type alternative. Second, while its costs would be lower, it would still double the costs of the current Social Security program. Finally, for those concerned about government involvement, this approach has the government picking the appropriate equity funds and retaining control of the money. This is not a particular problem in my view, but the TSP approach does raise all the same corporate governance issues as investment by the central Trust Funds.

Accumulating reserves in the Social Security Trust Funds and investing part of those reserves in equities is clearly superior to both the IRA-type and TSP approaches; it offers many of the advantages of privatized accounts without the risks and costs. It has the potential to increase national saving and offers participants the higher risk/higher returns associated with equity investment. But unlike privatized accounts, a partially funded Social Security program with equity investments ensures predictable retirement incomes by maintaining a defined-benefit structure that enables the sys-

tem to spread risks across the population and over generations. In addition, pooling investments keeps transaction
and reporting costs to a minimum, producing higher net
returns on equity investments than privatized accounts. Finally, by forcing participants to convert their funds into annuities, Social Security avoids the problem of adverse
selection and is in a good position to provide inflation-
adjusted benefits.

Investing the Trust Funds in equities is technically feasible. After all, in technical terms it is equivalent to investing
the same amount through privatized accounts. Indeed, a recent GAO report did not identify any insurmountable
hurdles associated with direct Trust-Fund investment.
Moreover, Trust-Fund investment as proposed by one
group of the Social Security Advisory Council should not
disrupt capital markets, since even by 2020 the Trust Funds
under this proposal would hold no more than 5 percent of
total equities outstanding. A portfolio shift of this magnitude would have only a minimal impact on interest rates
and federal interest expense.

Concern about government interference in private-sector
activity could be addressed through a careful structuring
of the investment arrangements, as Aaron suggests. This
would involve setting up an independent investment board,
investing in a broad index, and delegating voting rights to
fund managers. This arm's-length arrangement should en-
sure that the government is not directly influencing business
activity. It has worked very well for the federal TSP. Canada
will provide additional information, since it is in the process
of setting up a board that will oversee the Canadian Pension
Plan's investment in equities.

In short, investing the Trust Funds in equities is desirable on economic grounds, feasible in technical terms, and merits serious consideration. A partially funded defined-benefit plan can do everything that privatized accounts can do and do it at lower costs, yielding higher net returns.

A Realistic Assessment of Defined-Contribution Plans

In addition to refusing to consider equity investment by the central Trust Funds, Shoven starts out with a bias toward defined-contribution plans, which he views as stable arrangements that can more or less be put on automatic pilot. In contrast, he characterizes pay-as-you-go defined-benefit plans as "inherently financially unstable." The evidence suggests, however, that defined-contribution plans are no more stable than defined-benefit plans; the benefit promises under the two plans simply face different types of risks.

Larry Thompson of the Urban Institute carefully lays out these risks in a recent paper. Benefit promises under a classic defined-benefit plan are relatively insensitive to changes in the rate of wage growth or to changes in investment returns. On the other hand, future retirement benefits are very sensitive to demographic developments such as unanticipated changes in either the birth rate or retiree life spans. As we know from the current U.S. situation, an increase in the aged dependency ratio requires higher taxes, a later retirement age, or lower benefits.

Technically, the only benefit promise in a defined-contribution plan is that retirement income will reflect the assets accumulated by the time an individual retires. But the implicit promise is that contribution rates are set at a level such that the assets will produce enough income to hit a target replacement rate. In the defined-contribution model, retirement benefits are just as sensitive to unexpected changes in life expectancy as in the defined-benefit model. Without any change in contribution rates, longer life expectancies will result in lower annual benefits and therefore lower replacement rates.

Benefits under a defined-contribution plan are also very sensitive to economic developments such as changes in the rate of wage growth and changes in investment returns. Higher than expected investment returns reduce accumulations required to achieve a target replacement rate. Higher than expected wage growth increases the amount of required retirement income to achieve a target replacement rate and therefore increases the amount of required accumulations. Thus, the relationship between investment returns and wage growth is critical under a defined-contribution plan.

Wage growth and investment returns have varied significantly in the postwar period not only in the United States but also in the United Kingdom, Germany, and Japan. From 1953 to 1973, real wages grew very rapidly and real interest rates were quite low. In the post-1973 period, wage growth slowed in all four countries and real interest rates rose. In fact, real interest rates were consistently higher than real wage growth in all four countries through 1993.

The large variations in these economic variables would have had profound implications for contribution rates if defined-contribution plans had been in place. At some times, wage growth in these countries was so high relative to the real interest rate that the contribution required to hit a reasonable target replacement rate would have been 50 percent or more (e.g., the 1950s in Japan, Germany, and the United Kingdom and the 1960s in Japan). At other times, wage growth was so low relative to the level of interest rates that achieving the same replacement rate would have required a contribution rate of 10 percent (e.g., the 1970s and 1980s in the United States and the 1980s in Germany and Japan). Simulations over the entire postwar period suggest that even with reasonable rules for varying contribution rates, accumulations in defined-contribution plans would have fallen short of the target by as much as one-third or exceeded it by more than 100 percent. These misses would have translated immediately into benefits shortfalls or excesses.

In other words, defined-contribution plans cannot be put on automatic pilot if the government is trying to achieve a target replacement rate. Just like defined-benefit plans, they need adjustments in response to unexpected economic and demographic developments. The question is which pension model will produce the most effective government response. It is by no means clear that a defined-contribution plan would be better run and therefore more stable than a defined-benefit plan. My best guess is that imbalances will become evident more quickly under a defined-benefit plan and elicit more prompt government action.

Two Tiers and Efficiency

Nor is it clear that switching from a defined-benefit plan to a two-tier system with a defined-contribution component will improve efficiency. Shoven is not the first to argue that strengthening the link between benefits and contributions in the top tier will reduce the extent to which the payroll tax distorts labor supply decisions. But it is impossible to evaluate the merits of that hypothesis by simply looking at the defined-contribution component. The extent to which the payroll tax distorts labor supply decisions depends on the whole Social Security system, not just one part of it.

The two-tier approach trades a complicated and varying relationship between taxes and benefits under the existing system for two tiers—one where the benefit is more linked to taxes and one where it is less linked. In the extreme, Shoven and others propose a flat benefit for the bottom tier, which would make the payroll tax for that portion of the program purely distortionary. With one tier more linked and the other tier less linked, the two-tier approach would have the same amount of linkage on average as the current system, although the pattern would be different for different workers. Thus, there is no reason to think that the two-tier approach, considered as a whole, would be less distortionary than the current system.

A Tax Is a Tax Is a Tax

Finally, Shoven asserts that a tax is not a tax. That is, a government-mandated contribution is viewed as a tax if it finances a government-provided benefit based on previous earnings, but is not a tax if it finances a government-provided benefit based on the earnings on accumulated investments.

His assertion is almost certainly wrong. It implies that the mandated contribution to the defined-contribution portion of the program involves no distortions. That is unlikely. After all, the rationale for the current Social Security system is that individuals are myopic and would not save an adequate amount on their own. The fact that individuals would not undertake the saving voluntarily means that they undervalue it. As a result, they would probably view at least a portion of their top-tier contribution as an implicit tax.

More generally, if you asked most individuals if they view their FICA payment as a tax, they would undoubtedly say yes—even though they will inevitably get benefits based on these payments. The same would most likely be true for as mandatory payment to an account to which the taxpayer has no access until retirement. It would be foolhardy to construct policy on Shoven's assertion that a tax is not a tax.

Conclusion

Shoven recommends a defined-contribution component for Social Security because he fails to consider the advantages of the most realistic alternative—namely accumulating assets through the existing defined-benefit plan and investing some of those reserves in equities. He also mistakenly argues that a defined-contribution component will make the system efficient.

Shoven is right on one point. Two tiers, or even three tiers, are better than one. Defined-benefit and defined-contribution plans are subject to different types of risks. A system that combines the two approaches will function better than a system that relies on a single model. But the United States has never tried to provide retirement income through a single plan. By design, Social Security has provided inadequate income to middle- and upper-income individuals in the expectation that they will supplement these benefits on their own. It has worked, at least in part. Roughly 45 percent of the work force is covered by supplementary pensions. Many of these supplementary plans started as defined-benefit plans but increasingly have shifted to the defined-contribution model. On top of that, individuals can save independently through a variety of voluntary, tax-subsidized individual retirement accounts. In other words, the United States already has many tiers that combine the defined-benefit and defined-contribution approaches to providing retirement income. We do not have to privatize Social Security to create still another tier.

References

Advisory Council on Social Security. 1997. *Report of the 1994–1996 Advisory Council on Social Security.* Washington, D.C.: Government Printing Office.

Bohn, Henning. 1998. "Social Security Reform and Financial Markets." In Steven Sass and Robert Triest eds. *Social Security Reform: Links to Saving, Investment, and Growth.* Boston, MA: Federal Reserve Bank of Boston.

Diamond, Peter A. 1997. "Macroeconomic Aspects of Social Security Reform." *Brookings Papers on Economic Activity 2.*

Diamond, Peter A. Forthcoming. "Economics of Social Security Reform: An Overview." In R. Douglas Arnold, Michael Graetz, and Alicia H. Munnell eds. *Framing the Social Security Debate: Values, Politics, and Economics.* Washington, D.C.: National Academy of Social Insurance.

Hammond, P. Brett, and Mark J. Warshawsky. 1997. "Investing in Social Security Funds in Stocks." *Benefits Quarterly,* third quarter, 52–65.

Munnell, Alicia H., and Pierluigi Balduzzi. 1998. "Investing the Trust Funds in Equities." Washington, D.C.: Public Policy Institute, American Association of Retired Persons.

Peterson, Peter G. 1996. *Will America Grow Up Before It Grows Old?* New York: Random House.

Stein, Herbert. 1997. "Social Security and the Single Investor." *Wall Street Journal* (February 5).

Thompson, Lawrence H. Forthcoming. "Individual Uncertainty in Retirement Income Planning under Different Public Pension Regimes." in R. Douglas Arnold, Michael Graetz, and Alicia H. Munnell eds. *Framing the Social Security Debate: Values, Politics, and Economics.* Washington, D.C.: National Academy of Social Insurance.

United States General Accounting Office. 1998. *Social Security Investing: Implications of Government Stock Investing for the Trust Fund, the Federal Budget, and the Economy.* Washington, D.C.: Government Printing Office.

JAMES TOBIN

I was a student, disciple, and friend of Alvin Hansen. He was a great man, an inspiration to me as to others who knew him. It is a pleasure and privilege for me to be on this program, on a subject to which he made both scholarly and practical contributions. We are all indebted to Alvin Hansen's family and to Harvard for these symposia in his memory.

The Political Threat to Social Security

President Clinton has asked for a national debate this year on the future of Social Security. If the debate would match the high quality of the papers that Aaron and Shoven prepared for this symposium, we could be hopeful about the policy outcome. Right now, however,the greatest threat to Social Security as we know it is the campaign for extreme privatization, allowing workers to invest their payroll taxes for themselves in IRAs. As critics of Old Age and Survivors

Insurance (OASI) incessantly point out, those IRAs would very likely earn much higher returns on retirement than OASI can promise. If current payroll taxpayers opt out, the OASI Trust Fund won't be able to pay benefits due participants now retired or soon to retire. Advocates of privatization who entice workers with promises of stock market rates of return are inviting them to break the intergenerational compact on which the system depends.

These critics of Social Security also propose to convert OASI in whole or in large part into a defined-contribution (DC) pension system (like TIAA-CREF, beloved of academics). Social Security is instead a defined-benefit (DB) scheme. More important, it is social insurance, insurance against the general human risk of economic adversity in old age and incapacity to earn a living by employment. Social insurance requires universal participation, in which the premiums of the fortunate pay the claims of the unfortunate. This is the rationale for compulsory participation. Indeed, once society has recognized responsibility for aged citizens in distress, government has the right and duty to make sure that everyone who might benefit from this recognition makes provision against the contingency.

The advocates of extreme privatization and of full conversion to DC pensions would enable the more affluent to withdraw from Social Security as social insurance. An insurance system cannot survive the adverse selection of risks if the safest risks are allowed to opt out. The present DB system provides for progressivity in conversion of career payroll contributions into monthly pensions. These are entirely appropriate in social insurance, but would be difficult or impossible in a DC system. (Progressivity by federal subsidies augmenting each year missing or low payroll contributions are advocated in the DC plan of Kotlikoff and Sachs, but seem impractical.)

Demagogic and ideological delusions also threaten to wreck Medicare, which also depends on "community rating," in this case payment of insurance premiums by the healthy and affluent to pay the claims of the sick and poor.

The Rate of Return Must Be Raised

The young and affluent may be attracted to secession from social insurance because they misunderstand it. But it is understandable that they are dismayed by the rates of return their payroll taxes are likely to earn. Many cynically say that Social Security will not be there for them. OASI is largely a pay-as-you-go system, which in its pure form yields a rate of return in retirees' benefits over their earlier contributions just equal to the growth rate of the system's revenues, employment times real wages. The slowdowns beginning in the 1970s in both productivity growth and labor force growth presage puny rates of return to future retirees. In contrast, the elderly of the 1990s have benefited from high rates of growth of labor force and real wages and the expansion of the coverage of the system, now virtually complete.

As Aaron's paper shows, OASI can likely be saved in the sense of bridging the currently estimated gap, about 20 percent, between the present values of future revenues and future benefits. That can be done by a number of sensible and reasonable modifications of benefits while essentially preserving the present structure for most participants, for whom the replacement ratio of benefits to wages would stay about the same. Consequently, the absolute real value of baby boomers' Social Security pensions would be considerably higher than those of their parents. Nevertheless, the fact remains that on average the replacement ratio and the rate of return will be significantly lower in the future, especially for the young participants most vulnerable to the siren songs of the "reformers."

Raising Trust Fund Reserves and Diversifying Assets

Misgivings about the low rate of return on contributions is also the motive for proposals to invest at least some of these contributions in assets with a higher rate of return than government bonds, mainly common stocks. I don't recall any reform platform, DB or DC, that does not include this plank. Aaron is counting on diversifying the trust fund into stock market securities to fill 35 to 45 percent of the gap. He would bring common stocks up to 40 percent of reserves by 2015. The question is how big the reserves will be then and subsequently.

After all, rates of return on Trust Fund assets matter only to the extent that the Trust Fund has net assets. In a pure pay-as-you-go system that balance is negligible, and the return is just the growth rate of the system. Thanks to the 1983 Greenspan-O'Neill-Reagan reforms, so scathingly condemned by Shoven, we now have a nonnegligible and growing Trust Fund. In 1997 its assets were 165 percent of outlays; they will rise to 350 percent by 2010. But reserves will stop growing about 2013 and will be exhausted in 2032. If reform now would keep the inflow at a significant ratio to total annual benefit payments, improvements in Trust Fund earnings would make a big difference. This is a good reason for putting into effect as promptly as possible, long before they are urgently needed, many modifications of benefits and other reforms listed by Aaron and Shoven.

President Clinton's proposal, in the context of the politics of disposition of prospective budget surpluses, to "save Social Security first" should be taken seriously. I take a meaningful interpretation to be that, in addition to the Trust Fund's own surplus, any surplus in the unified budget would be appropriated to the credit of the OASDI Trust Funds, that is, become a debt of the Treasury to the Trust Funds. (I realize that this means that part or all of the Trust Funds' own surplus might thus be counted twice. This is, like much other budget accounting, a political gimmick, for a better cause than most such gimmicks. Less generous to Social Security would be to credit any on-budget surplus to the Trust Funds.) The Trust Funds would invest these amounts in private stock and bond funds, owned and managed by the Trust Funds, not by individuals.

The larger the multiple of their liabilities the balances in the Trust Funds are, the greater the degree to which the pensions will reflect the Trust Funds' earnings, relative to the minimal pure pay-as-you-go payoff. In the extreme, fully funded case, participants would earn the rate of return to the Trust Funds portfolios less minimal administrative costs.

Funding? A Second Tier?

The vulnerability of the pay-as-you-go system to adverse demographic and economic shocks brought the problems of

Social Security with which we are now struggling. OASI had developed into a DB pension plan and it became difficult and painful to find revenues to assure payments of the benefits defined. This was one reason for the growing popularity of DC plans, yielding whatever benefits could be paid from the accumulation of contributions.

Funding and DC, however, are not the same thing. The system could be funded in aggregate and distribute as retirement benefits only the income on the aggregate fund built up from its contributions. In this way, progressivity in the formula connecting contributions to benefits, as exists now, could be continued. For the participants, it would be a DB system, but periodic revision of benefits would be taken as normal rather than as a sign of crisis.

Likewise, the buildup of reserves, discussed above, would result in a partially funded, partially pay-as-you-go DB system.

An advantage of individualized DC accounts is to tie contributions and future retirement benefits tightly together in the participant's consciousness. Too often today workers regard Social Security contributions as burdensome taxes and don't connect them with the benefits they will eventually receive. Shoven points out that looseness in this identification makes payroll taxes bigger disincentives to work. (On the other hand, participants' skepticism that Social Security will "be there for me" might encourage private and national saving.)

Shoven rightly criticizes the annual financial accounts the Social Security Administration (SSA) now reports to its clients. Their flaws could an be substantially remedied without moving to DC.

It would take a half century to install a fully funded system, individualized or aggregate. During the transition the working generations would have to support the elderly Social Security beneficiaries of the present pay-as-you-go system while also building up in advance the funds that would generate their own pensions. The extra national saving in this process would in principle supply additional national real capital, partially replacing the workers lost in the demographic slowdown. Kotlikoff and Sachs propose to accomplish this transition by a general federal sales tax.

Attention of more practical reformers has focused on what Shoven calls two-tier systems, with universal DC schemes supplementing but not replacing, at least not wholly replacing, the present DB OASI system. I am sympathetic to a second tier and I do not think the more modest of these proposals are so distant from Aaron's reformed one-tier DB system with augmented reserves invested in diversified portfolios.

As Aaron reminds us, there is no obvious differential advantage in economy-wide saving and investment in one or another of three possibilities: (1) individuals are refunded taxes and buy private securities, (2) the SSA buys private securities for each individual's account with his or her taxes, (3) the SSA buys private securities for its aggregate Trust Fund reserves. In all cases, the rest of the economy sells those securities and buys in their place the government bonds the Trust Fund would otherwise have held. The swap might be welfare-improving, however, if the OASI beneficiaries end up with higher yielding assets. Even though these are also riskier, they diversify the portfolios of less affluent workers and retirees in a desirable direction.

For Gramlich' s Individual Accounts Plan

Among the plans reviewed by Shoven, my vote goes to the Individual Account (IA) proposal of another of my students, Ned Gramlich. I would gradually move the required percentage of covered earnings up from his 1.6 percent to the Committee for Economic Development's 4.0. Also, I would welcome voluntary additional subscriptions, by workers or by employers, on their behalf. The IA and CED plans are really second tiers. The forced saving levies that finance them are additional to present payroll taxes; the plans are not substitutes for current OASI. They really can contribute to a net increase in national saving, unlike proposals to carve DC accounts out of traditional Social Security.

It is essential, in my opinion, that these new DC individual accounts be held and managed by the SSA, or by the new independent board Aaron proposes, that choices be confined to a few index funds, and that accounts be annuitized on retirement. I believe that fully privatized compulsory DC plans, with individuals investing for themselves hounded by mutual fund salespeople, would be a disastrous and expensive mess. I would reject any plan that one way or another, on whatever terms, makes payroll taxes cashable, or offers income tax credits, or creates IRAs, or goes into debt for most of a century. Besides their many other questionable features, Moynihan, Feldstein, and the two personal security account plans strike me as what the English call "too clever by half."

I was relieved that in the end Shoven ranked CED first, ahead of his own variant of the personal security accounts proposal, though I prefer his rank number 5, Gramlich's individual accounts plan, to CED's proposal.

4   Responses

JOHN B. SHOVEN

I want to thank Henry Aaron for offering such a spirited defense of continuing the single-tier defined benefit structure of the Social Security system and the four discussants for their thoughtful remarks and helpful ideas. My view about the desirability of adopting a two-tier program for Social Security is, if anything, strengthened by this symposium. After the majority of the members of the Advisory Council on Social Security advocated one form or other of a supplementary defined-contribution tier to Social Security, the majority of the distinguished discussants at today's panel did likewise. As I count heads, Tobin, Cutler, and Barro all favor some form of individual accounts over simply trying to repair the existing defined-benefit Social Security system once more.[1] The score is three-to-one, which is a little stronger than the seven-to-five count on the Advisory Council.

There are many reasons for favoring the two-tier approach. First, all three of my top ranked two-tier plans offer substantially more benefits for retirees than Aaron's menu of reforms or the Advisory Council's "maintain benefits" (MB) plan. Why? The basic reason is that all of the two-tier plans involve higher contributions or revenues. In particular, the CED plan and the IA plan collect essentially the same payroll tax revenue as the Aaron and MB plans, but they use the revenue only to fund their tier-one benefits. Their defined contribution plans are supplementary (with contribution rates of 3.0 and 1.6 percent of covered payroll, respectively) and will in all likelihood provide benefits that at least offset the benefit cuts required to bring about financial solvency. Aaron and the MB advocates have no supplementary plan to fill in the gap left by their benefit cuts (such as advancing the retirement age). Aaron's 0.4 percent payroll tax increase is simply not enough to match the CED or IA plans (or my version of the PSA plan) all of which raise mandatory contribution rates from 1.6 or 3.0 percent. Restoring the financial solvency of Social Security while providing adequate retirement benefits for future generations requires more money—more than currently legislated and more than Aaron is proposing.

Second, and closely related, all of the promising hybrid plans involve more national saving than the Aaron menu of reforms or the MB plan. In principle, as Munnell and Cutler point out in their remarks and as Aaron stresses in his paper, a funded defined-benefit plan could contribute just as much to national saving as a supplementary defined-contribution plan. But, none of the advocates of the single-tier DB approach are willing to raise taxes as much as my three preferred plans raise required contribution rates. Because of this, they do not measure up in terms of potential to increase national saving.

Even if we choose to dramatically increase the saving generated by a DB plan by raising payroll tax rates substantially and accumulating an enormous Trust Fund, there is a serious question (raised by Barro in the discussion) about whether politicians could resist eroding the fund by either lowering taxes or raising benefits. Is it really feasible and credible for the government to commit to saving for society with a massive Trust Fund?—history is not very reassuring. It is my judgment that Barro is right and that saving in individual accounts is much more sustainable than saving centrally.

Another advantage of supplementary individual accounts is that people can hold safe or risky portfolios depending on their attitudes toward risk. If the government is going to increase the riskiness of Trust Fund investments by placing 40 percent of the portfolio in equity markets (as Aaron advocates), then individuals (particularly poor individuals) have no choice but to participate. Why do we think that "one size fits all" is the right answer for this type of investment? Why not give people choices?

I agree with Aaron and Munnell that the basic Social Security pension plan should result in an inflation-indexed life annuity. The CED plan would do this as would the Feldstein-Samwick plan, my version of the PSA plan (on the 2.5 percent government contribution to tier two), and even the Moynihan plan. All of the two-tier plans would annuitize the first tier of payouts. So, what is the issue here? We all are in agreement.

In terms of management expenses, I believe that we need to be imaginative. I do not support an environment as unregulated as the present IRA/401(k) one. The government could and should offer a federal TSP type of account and can probably do so for the 10 basis points estimated by the Advisory Council. The question is whether that should be the only game in town. My current opinion is "no." I think that it would be preferable to allow private mutual fund companies who meet appropriateness regulations and who impose management fees below some prescribed amount— such as 75 basis points—to compete with the government. Perhaps the appropriateness regulations would require all offerings to be broad-based indexed funds. More thought needs to be given to this subject. The fact that the current federal Thrift Savings Plan does not allow participants to invest in foreign securities (and therefore denies the participants the extra diversification of a global portfolio) is a factor in my preferring a more open competitive environment. The government almost certainly could not resist politically influencing the portfolios as they apparently have with the federal Thrift Savings Plan.

Many private employers have adopted supplementary defined-contribution plans to their basic defined-benefits pension programs. Everyone agrees that the choice between plan types is not a choice between a "safe" program and a "risky" one, but rather that both types of plans involve risks, albeit of a different nature. Economic theory and common sense tell us in such circumstances to choose a "some of each" strategy rather than put all of our eggs in one basket. The hybrid plans that I advocate in my paper offer attractive "some of each" combinations for a Social Security program for the twenty-first century. When I add up all the considerations, I find that the arguments to reform Social Security by adopting a two-tier system are quite overwhelming. Two-tiers are better than one because of risk diversification for participants, more saving for the country, more choice for households, and more retirement benefits for the elderly.

Note

1. Tobin explicitly advocates an enlarged IA plan with second-tier contribution rates eventually reaching 4.0 percent. I count Cutler in the CED camp and Barro as consistently favoring more privatization. Only Munnell supports Aaron and the MB approach.

HENRY J. AARON

I want to begin my response by calling attention to the broad agreement among us on certain fundamental questions.

• We all agree that privatization *per se* does nothing to raise national saving, investment, or economic growth.

• We also agree that, for any given level of national saving, the nation's growth path does not depend on whether the reserves to back up this basic pension are managed by the Social Security trustees or by individuals. This point deserves emphasis, because many others make opposite arguments. In Cutler's words: their claims are simply incorrect.

• All of us, other than Barro, agree that measures to promote national saving—through increased taxes or reduced government spending—would be desirable, although we appear to have different readings on just how much taxes should rise.

Shoven explicitly ranks highest those reform plans that raise taxes most. Tobin looks forward to raising payroll taxes 4 percentage points. Cutler wants higher taxes, too. I proposed a plan that would restore long-term financial balance that depended on only a small tax increase because I am convinced that a tax-phobic American public will not support large tax increases. I also think that it is important at this point in a very serious debate to talk about plans that have some chance of acceptance. Large tax increases have none. There is a time for academic speculation about hypothetical policies for imaginary worlds. Things have gotten real, however, so let us be real.

Under some interpretations, of course, depriving people of the right to spend income currently is not a tax—the individual keeps title, right? Well, not quite. The plans Shoven embraces force people to set aside even more of current income than current payroll taxes do. Workers would not have use of their funds for a few decades on the average, the same delay as under Social Security. I know of no economist who does not regard forced saving schemes as a tax at least in part, because individuals are forced to use their incomes for something that they preferred not to use it for. I also know of no better definition of the word "tax" than "government action to require people to use their income for something that they did not want to use it for." Let us be straightforward. The essence of social insurance, through Social Security or through individual accounts, is the imposition of—listen closely—"taxes" to raise funds to make sure that people have adequate incomes sometime in the future under stipulated situations.

But, more substantively, all individual account plans would return less to individuals than would a reformed Social Security system, for any given level of taxes. Both arrangements can invest in the same assets. Both pay benefits after an average delay of a few decades. The only real difference, apart from who bears the risk, is that individual accounts will generate higher administrative costs that eat up investment income which remains available to support pensions under Social Security. For an economist, that is the real tax—or, more precisely, the real "excess burden"—the needless administrative costs under individual accounts that erode funds available to individuals.

My main point, however, is that the size of the optimal tax increase is not germane to our debate. Whatever the total resources available to support the goal of assuring Americans adequate basic incomes to retirees, the disabled, and survivors, one must decide on the *best way* to provide that support. Whether or not Shoven, Tobin, and Cutler can find 51 senators, 218 representatives, and a president willing to approve large tax increases, we must still answer the same question: *what is the best vehicle for converting those taxes into pensions?* Most of us agree that complete privatization is a bad idea and that even partial privatization through individual accounts modeled on individual retirement accounts (IRAs) would be cumbersome, costly, and inadvisable. Shoven appears to regard with equanimity the nearly 20 *percent* loading charge, which is equivalent to the 0.75 percent annual cost for fund management that he thinks might result if people could choose fiduciaries freely. He does not explain why he thinks this projection is plausible for deposits that would be $30 or less per month under his plan for approximately 70 million workers, particularly since actual annual management charges on much larger accounts in stock mutual funds now average 1.21 to 1.25 percent and have *risen* over the past decade.[1] Nor does he explain why it helps worker-pensioners to expose them to such costs for a program designed to ensure that they receive a basic income.

• I am sure that we would all also agree that the current debate on how to modify Social Security is *not* about whether people should have access to tax sheltered savings. Virtually every American already enjoys such access— through IRAs, Keogh plans, 401(k) plans, or one of the many other tax-sheltered saving programs that Congress has enacted over the past twenty years.

• All of us agree that workers should have access to the extra returns provided by investments in common stocks—the so-called "equity premium"—although we disagree on the institutional framework within which that return should be secured.

What is at issue, therefore, are two questions:

• Whether a defined-benefit or a defined-contribution system will better achieve the principal goal of a government mandated saving program—to assure basic pension coverage to retirees, the disabled, and survivors.

• Whether the prospects of assuring pensioners access to the equity premium and raising national saving are better if funds are administered by private funds managers hired by

Social Security trustees, or by private funds managers hired by individual account holders.

The key words in the first question are *assure* and *basic*. We all agree that individuals can not and should not depend exclusively on social insurance. Private pensions and individual saving are necessary supplements. We also agree that a civilized nation cannot permit the elderly, disabled, or survivors to live in indigence. One could provide such income exclusively through means-tested benefits. All of us oppose this approach. Australia is the only developed nation that provides pensions exclusively in this form. (Even Barro recognizes that some form of mandatory saving is necessary, which is worth noting because he appears unable to understand that it makes sense for him, as a rich and much recruited professor, consultant, and columnist, to pay more in payroll taxes than his mother receives in benefits, so that others less fortunate than he can receive a bit of social assistance without a means test.) Australia also has the highest poverty rate among the elderly of any developed country. Every other developed nation provides earnings-related social insurance benefits. There appears to be an international consensus that people should be assured something more than bare subsistence when they retire or become disabled and that what they receive should vary with income, although perhaps less than proportionately.

If the goal of social insurance is to *assure* a basic income, all of Shoven's arguments about the advantages of allowing individuals to select portfolios that reflect their attitudes toward risk are simply irrelevant. If our goal is to make sure that people achieve a basic income *with certainty*, authorizing people to assume various levels of risk, with attendant variations in rates of return in each person's portfolio, defeats that basic purpose of the program. What sense does it make to give people the right to take risks that may cause their incomes to fall below the level that it is the program's basic purpose to guarantee? The answer is simple: *it makes no sense at all*. With respect to voluntary saving, in contrast, individual risk bearing with commensurate returns, is essential to the proper functioning of private capital markets. Such risk bearing elicits better decisions on how much to save *voluntarily* and what to invest in than any other device that has been developed.

Risk in long-term contracts, such as pensions, however, is inescapable. There is no way to erase the risks inherent in fluctuations of asset prices, variations in wage growth, unforeseen demographic trends, or unexpected inflation. Somebody has to bear those risks. So the practical question is: who? It is telling that neither Shoven nor any of the respondents, other than Munnell, seriously examined this central question.

Under defined-benefit plans, risks are political. When a plan goes out of financial balance, legislatures act in one of two ways. *Responsible* legislatures promptly raise or lower benefits or taxes, usually distributing the benefits (in the case of surpluses) or costs (in the case of deficits) broadly and gradually among workers and current and future pensioners—through changed taxes and benefits for current and future beneficiaries. In this way, individual workers and cohorts are spared the shock of sharp variations in income. *Irresponsible* legislatures procrastinate or take steps that make later adjustments even more difficult. The result is crisis and, in some countries, collapse of the social insurance system.

Under defined-contribution plans, risks arise from fluctuations in asset prices, unexpected inflation, unemployment, or other sources. Workers who retire just after asset prices have fallen or when interest rates are low will find that their savings are reduced and can buy smaller annuities than they anticipated. They bear these risks directly.

The question for any society is how to handle these risks in the best possible way. The answer is not a matter of ideology. It depends on national facts and circumstances. These facts and circumstances include national political stability, a record of responsible behavior by government, and the existence of financial institutions capable of handling private accounts. What does experience in the United States indicate about how best to make sure that individuals receive assured, basic benefits?

In my view, the U.S. record in handling social insurance has been and remains exemplary. The United States made seventy-five-year projections before any other nation did. It has invariably taken measures to restore projected long-term financial balance within a few years after the system has fallen out of "close actuarial balance" (defined as revenues outside the range of 95 to 100 percent of projected outlays). Not one Social Security check has ever been delayed. Replacement rates have been remarkably stable, varying by no more than 5 percentage points since before automatic adjustments for inflation were enacted in 1972. For many years, a consensus held that Social Security should be financed on a pay-as-you-go basis, but when that consensus changed, Congress set benefit and tax schedules in place that have led to reserves of more than $700 billion and they are projected to continue rising for two decades until they exceed $3.7 trillion. All of us in this debate would like to see those reserves rise faster and further than projected under current law. In the current climate, the prospects for achieving that result are excellent.

The record of stability in private financial markets cannot come close to that achieved by Social Security. Stock prices have fluctuated over wide ranges, falling by approximately half during the rolling financial depression spanning the 1970s. Bond prices have been periodically hammered by rising nominal interest rates.

Social Security has been a major league success in assuring stable incomes to the retired, disabled, and survivors. By comparison, the record of defined-contribution accounts in providing *stable* benefits has been bush league. There is no prospect that events will cause any change in this judgment in the future. This view is not one of enthusiasm for 1960s government programs that all adults should have outgrown, as Barro snidely observes—it is simple fact, unencumbered by ideology.

The second question concerns how to design an institutional framework for assuring pensioners access to the equity premium and, if possible, boosting the national saving rate. My own view is that any attempt to raise national saving—by creating individual accounts or accumulating Trust Fund reserves—is subject to erosion.

Individuals who find themselves with a new asset called an "individual account" can cut back private saving, increase consumer borrowing, maintain larger mortgages, or pressure employers to shift compensation away from retirement benefits to cash wages or current fringe benefits. The record with tax-sheltered "retirement saving" indicates that Congress has no spine to resist "early withdrawals"—to buy a home, to finance education, to pay for illness, or whenever one changes a job. I have no doubt that creating private accounts would boost saving by some proportion of the total accumulation, but those who think that gross accumulations even come close to net accumulations are living in a dream world.

Similarly, I have no doubt that adding to Social Security Trust Fund reserves will boost saving, but by less than gross additions to the Trust Funds. Institutional safeguards can limit the erosion, but probably not eliminate it. Among the safeguards, the following steps should be taken:

• Congress should require all budget reporting to exclude pension fund accounts from the budget for ordinary operations. The government is the fiduciary for the nation's basic retirement program. Budget resolutions and all budget reporting should be based on operations of government other than Social Security. The "unified budget" would be consigned to "special analyses."

• Congress should create a Social Security Reserve Board (SSRB) along the lines described in my initial presentation.

• Congress should require that the SSRB administer Social Security to meet financial standards, including minimum reserves, similar to those which the Employee Retirement Income Security Act imposes on private pension plans. The SSRB should be required to report on whether any proposed legislation would retard achievement of those reserve standards. A super-majority of SSRB members would have to certify that any proposed Social Security legislation did not retard achievement of the target financial standards. Without such *imprimatur*, legislation would require a super-majority to pass in the Senate, be subject to points of order in the House, and confront other procedural obstacles.

I *think*, but am not confident, that such safeguards would make it a better-than-even-money bet that accumulation of Trust Fund reserves would boost national saving at least as much as would accumulations in individual accounts. But I am *sure* that the difference would be small. Given such a difference, I am quite willing to see my children become only 50 percent richer than I am, rather than 55 percent, if that is the price to retain a pension system that spares those who have meager income or little financial knowledge exposure to the risk that a drop in asset prices or real interest rates will undercut their retirement or disability benefits. Wouldn't you be willing to make that trade, too?

Note

1. Robert McGough, "Robust Fund Industry Isn't Lowering Fees," *Wall Street Journal*, May 14, 1998, C1.

5   Rejoinder

John B. Shoven

I remain convinced that the best way to reform Social Security is to introduce a two-part system that combines the advantages of defined-benefit and defined-contribution systems. In this very brief rejoinder, however, I want to take issue with only one aspect of Aaron's *Response*. He states that I favor plans that raise taxes the most, that Tobin looks forward to raising payroll taxes by 4 percentage points, and that Cutler also wants higher taxes. These statements are simply not accurate. None of us desire higher taxes or even propose higher taxes. What we desire and propose are measures to bring about higher personal and national savings. We propose mandatory individual saving accounts as a second tier in the Social Security program. Payments to your own account, even if mandatory, are not taxes. The money is held in your name and will benefit you and / or your beneficiaries. You manage the money and receive quarterly statements about its status. To differentiate this program from a tax increase, simply ask yourself when the government allowed you to designate how you would like your taxes invested for your benefit. The answer, of course, is "never."

When you pay taxes, you give up title to the money and cannot control how it is spent. The new second tier that Tobin and Cutler and I (and the majority of the Social Security Advisory Council) propose for Social Security should be thought of as a mandatory defined-contribution pension plan. That is what it is—and it is not a tax. In fact, my top ranked plan, termed "Shoven's variant on the PSA plan" involves a tax cut. The payroll deductions of workers would rise from 12.4 percent of covered wages to 14.9 percent, but slightly over one-third of the money, 5.0 percent of payroll, would be directed to individual accounts. Only the remaining 9.9 percent of payroll can accurately be termed a tax. Workers do not think of existing contributions to pension plans as taxes; there is no reason to think of the proposed second tier of Social Security differently. There may be arguments against establishing individual accounts as part of Social Security. Calling the contributions to these accounts taxes, however, is misleading. The plans I like the most involve the most saving and we all know that increasing saving requires setting additional money aside—extra contributions to accounts. I advocate these two-tier plans partly because they do not involve tax increases.

Contributors

Henry J. Aaron
Bruce and Virginia
MacLaury Senior Fellow
The Brookings Institution

Robert J. Barro
Robert C. Waggoner
Professor of Economics
Harvard University

David M. Cutler
Professor of Economics
Harvard University

Benjamin M. Friedman
William Joseph Maier
Professor of Political
Economy
Harvard University

Alicia H. Munnell
Peter F. Drucker Professor
of Management Sciences
Carroll School of
Management
Boston College

John B. Shoven
Charles R. Schwab
Professor of Economics and
Vernon and Lysbeth
Anderson Dean of
Humanities and Science
Stanford University

James Tobin
Sterling Professor of
Economics Emeritus
Yale University

Index